Love Goes to Press

Love
Goes to
Press

[*A Comedy in Three Acts*] by MARTHA GELLHORN *and* VIRGINIA COWLES.
With an Introduction by MARTHA GELLHORN. *Edited*
with an Afterword by SANDRA SPANIER.
University of Nebraska Press
Lincoln and London

Library of Congress Cataloging in Publication Data.
Gellhorn, Martha, 1908–
    Love goes to press: a comedy in three acts / by Martha Gellhorn
    and Virginia Cowles; with an introduction by Martha Gellhorn;
    edited with an afterword by Sandra Spanier.
    p.   cm.
    ISBN 0-8032-2154-1 (alk. paper).
    1. World War, 1939–1945—Drama.   I. Cowles, Virginia.
    II. Spanier, Sandra Whipple, 1951– .   III. Title.
    PS3513.E46L68   1995
    812'.54—dc20
    94-22925
    CIP

Contents

Introduction by Martha Gellhorn   vii

Editor's Note   xiii

Love Goes to Press: *A Comedy in Three Acts*
   by Martha Gellhorn and Virginia Cowles   1

Afterword by Sandra Spanier   79

ILLUSTRATIONS FOLLOWING PAGE 78

Photo from Broadway opening, 1947

Illustration previewing U.S. opening, 1946

Gellhorn and Cowles, 1946

Gellhorn at Thunderbolt base, Germany, 1945

Gellhorn at Borinquen Field, Puerto Rico, 1942

Gellhorn, Cuba, 1941

Cowles, London, c.1941

Introduction

I must advise you at once that this play bears no resemblance whatever, of any kind at all, to war and war correspondents. It is a joke. It was intended to make people laugh and make money. It made people laugh splendidly in London; however, not a penny was received by the playwrights, my friend Ginny (Virginia Cowles) and me. That remains a puzzle, but perhaps not having a contract, due to our ignorance, explains it. We knew nothing about the theater; it was not our line of work. We were barely playgoers. The history of this play now strikes me as a bigger joke than the play.

One feature of our comedy is authentic: the squalid stage sets. No stage is small enough to give a true impression of the cubicles called rooms in the little beat-up brick house in the beat-up village of Sessa Aurunca, the press camp we used as a model. Press camp merely meant any place the press was told to live and given means of sending copy to their editors. Sessa Aurunca was the only press camp I lived in during World War II, the only time I had correct travel orders to allow me the privilege. Conditions in our Italian hovel reached such a high point of awfulness that it was fun, memorable after fifty years.

Sessa Aurunca lies about fifteen miles south of Cassino, where the Italian campaign had ground to a halt. The Germans held the dominating ancient fortress monastery of Monte Cassino, blocking the road to Rome. The Italian campaign was fought by two armies, the American Fifth Army and the British Eighth Army, a marvelous polyglot throng that included the tall, feared black North African goums attached to the Free French, Poles, Gurkhas, Canadians, and all types of Britons. In principle the Fifth Army operated on the west side of Italy and the Eighth Army to the east, but in practice there was interweaving. In March 1944, our scruffy press camp was under Eighth Army command while American infantry had dug itself into shelves in the hillside below the monastery.

Apart from useless erratic artillery fire, there was no action and nothing to write about, but this was the only Allied front in the war, and four American male correspondents were stuck in Sessa Aurunca, by editors' orders, for as long as the unfortunate American troops were stuck into that hillside. The press camp was run by a darling loopy British officer who had been blown out of his tank, the sole survivor, and was assigned the job of handling correspondents as a strange sort of rest cure.

Ginny breezed in from London, via Army HQ at Caserta near Naples, to see me and some chums in a British tank outfit stationed nearby. Though fearless, she had tired of the discomfort of following troops after a long spell in the Western Desert, the year before. Now she was an admired think-piece writer for the *London Telegraph* and had already collected the high-level stuff she wanted from the Commanding General at Caserta. She spent most of her short visit cadging food from the press camp kitchen to feed the hungry village kids. Nobody wanted to go anywhere with me after I wheedled two colleagues into chancing the open, unpleasantly silent road that led to the Americans' position beneath the monastery. I needed them to make the full load that justified getting transport. Our jeep on the empty road attracted a couple of German mortar shells which bounced us into the ditches. No one liked ditches in Italy because of mines. Usually I bumped along the churned side roads with a driver to call on other American troops resting under wet canvas, in mud to their boot tops, waiting to go back to the detested hillside. The staple weather was cold rain.

In the evening, Ginny and I larked about, probably irritating our colleagues since we could leave when we wanted and they could not. But the darling British officer thought us a welcome treat. We had the setting for our play, and a shared experience. I should add that I met Ginny in Madrid during the Spanish war. Ginny made London her permanent home after Spain, and we had both reported on war in various countries since then. That is all the background you need.

In the early summer of 1945, after the war ended in Europe, Ginny and I were in London, feeling aimless like millions of others. Though no one spoke of it, sorrow affected me; now there was time to think of the heart-sickening cost of the war. Nothing seemed worth the effort of doing it. Ginny, more energetic, dreamed up this brilliant idea. We would write a jokey play about war correspondents. After a successful run in London, the play would be bought by the movies, bringing us pots of money, of which neither of us had much. I said no, it's silly, we don't know how to write a play, not even how to begin. Ginny observed that I might as well try it, since I was clearly unemployed. All right, but how long is a play, for instance?

The simple solution, buy a printed play and check it for length, did not occur to us. Instead we went to a matinée with free tickets from the star, a friend of Ginny's, taking a stopwatch along. We timed the acts. After this weird beginning, we each wrote a page of double-spaced dialogue with a few stage instructions (such as "enter from right") thrown in, and read the page aloud, again with a stopwatch. Word counting and timing and childish arithmetic gave us the basic information: how many pages of double-spaced typing were needed per act.

Then we discussed the play. Ginny had all the ideas for the plot. I kept objecting that they were too ridiculous, a joke is a joke but this is absurd farce. As I had no plot ideas myself, that was that. We figured out roughly what was to happen in each act, or rather Ginny did while I made more objections, and proceeded, in our separate dwellings, to write the acts. No matter how dotty the content, I loved writing dialogue. I think we spent ten days on it, and it would have been quicker except for arguments. It was a pushover: just dialogue, people running on and off the stage, you didn't have to describe anything or anybody. We patched our two versions together with cellotape, a bit of Ginny's, a bit of mine. The two female leads, Jane and Annabelle, were caricatures of Ginny and me. It is very long ago, but I believe that Ginny wrote most of Annabelle (me) and I wrote most of Jane (Ginny). The male characters were not caricatures of anybody, pure and improbable figments of the imagination.

When the play was all pasted together, we asked another friend of Ginny's (Ginny knew everyone in London), a beautiful young actress named Penelope Dudley Ward, to read it aloud so that we could get a notion of how it sounded. Some of the dialogue made Pempie laugh so hard that she couldn't read, which we took as a good sign. Neither of us doubted for a moment that the play would be performed.

This giant act of creation completed, I went back to work, hanging around with the 82nd Airborne, the American occupying force in Berlin. Ginny stayed in London and must have found an agent because the next news was that the play was being rehearsed with an odious title, "Love Goes to Press," tacked on by whoever bought the script. We were never consulted and did not think we had any rights. I remember being distressed by the title, saying that it made the play even more ludicrous, but Ginny pointed out that playwriting was not our business.

The director of "Love Goes to Press" was a young man who had gained his directorial experience from putting on countless amateur theatricals during his years in a German prisoner of war camp. The male characters had all served in the war, so they could use their old uniforms. The girl who played Jane had never acted in a real theater but on many makeshift platforms, as part of an ENSA troupe. ENSA was the official British entertainment organization that sent actors and singers all over Britain and Europe where British forces were being bored and miserable in reserve billets. She also had a uniform. Annabelle was Irene Worth, fresh from California, in her first role on the British stage. Our play was a super bargain to produce: no money for costumes, a little loose cash for pieces of tatty secondhand furniture, and the unknown young director and actors charmed by whatever salary was offered.

We did not know that playwrights are supposed to attend rehearsals and show interest and be helpful. We saw the play for the first time on its opening night at the Embassy Theatre in Swiss Cottage, North

London, a sizeable equivalent to off-Broadway theaters. We sat in the balcony with Ginny's new husband and my old friend, Aidan Crawley. The actors were fresh and lively, and the audience roared with laughter. After the final curtain, with the cast lined up on the stage, there were cries of "Author! Author!" Ginny and Aidan and I fled from the balcony into the night. We also did not know that authors are supposed to make a gracious little speech when the audience is applauding loudly and calling out for them.

The play ran for weeks at Swiss Cottage, though we never went back to see it, and then moved to the Duchess Theatre in London's West End. We were not surprised or elated by this; according to Ginny's scheme, it would now play in London for a time until being bought by the movies. We went once to see it at the Duchess Theatre but did not think it our place to go backstage and congratulate the actors; we would not have wanted to intrude.

The trouble was that the audiences laughed too much, and this convinced an American producer that he should take the play to New York. Everyone in those London audiences knew about real war; they had lived through it, either in uniform or as embattled civilians. Knowing the real thing, they were free to laugh at this comic, unreal version of war. Everyone longed to laugh in the first cold winter of peace. Everyone was tired, and peace did not bring any letup in daily hardship. London looked terrible, bombed, shabby, and there was nothing to buy except utility clothes and utility furniture, and scant unappealing food, all on ration cards. Laughter was lifesaving escape. Theater tickets were inexpensive, and a theater was warm because of all the bodies in it. New York was something else.

As usual, nobody asked our opinion; we were simply informed that the play was going overseas. The cast was beside itself with joy. New York looked like heaven. At last they could eat immensely and shop; Jane would buy silk stockings and good cosmetics and some pretty clothes; the men had their own priorities, possibly just an unlimited supply of drink and cigarettes. And they would all be warm and comfortable: bliss. Only Irene Worth refused to go. She announced that she was staying in London where one day she would play Shakespeare. Ginny told me this and I thought it the daftest ambition I had ever heard, but look what happened.

The play lasted four days in New York. We gathered that the critics were furious with it. Since they had not lived through real war, they found it outrageous, tasteless, grotesque, practically wicked to make cheap jokes about any aspect of war. That was the end of the play.

At this late date, I have finally read an actual 1947 review. An American postgraduate student dug it up like an archeological find and sent it to me in her thesis. The review is so solemn, angry, and enjoyable that it is worth quoting. Rosamond Gilder of *Theater Arts* wrote,

> *Love Goes to Press*, written by two war correspondents, is, one hopes, a libel on the profession. If this is the way Martha Gellhorn and Virginia Cowles themselves behaved in the pursuit of their newspaper assignments, it would seem wise for the high command to banish all women journalists from the next war. Presumably the whole affair was supposed to be funny but since their writing lacks wit and their plotting any elements of conviction one is driven back to a criticism of the content of the play and the strange ethics as well as the incredible human callousness exhibited by the characters they portrayed.

There you are: some jokes, like some white wines, do not travel.

When news of this extreme failure arrived, Ginny was in London, busy being newly married. I was in Portugal, in search of sun and food while I worked on a war novel. I have discovered a diary of that time, thin greyish rationed paper, written in pencil so that I can hardly read it. For one day in early January 1947, I was badly upset and sorry for the cast unless they could find jobs that kept them in New York. There is no mention of the play the next day or any day afterwards. I was fretting over my novel and dismayed by rain.

Some years later, Ginny wanted me to write another play with her about the House of Commons where Aidan was a member of Parliament. I said, flatly, never again; there is no future in get-rich schemes, and besides, I only like the movies.

Martha Gellhorn

Editor's Note

Far ahead of its time in its comic depiction of men and women at war, *Love Goes to Press* is now a fascinating piece of literary history, still fresh and funny after fifty years. In the summer of 1992, I suggested to Martha Gellhorn that, in light of current reevaluations of the literary canon and the politics of literary reputation and a growing interest in women's war writing, the World War II play that she wrote with her fellow war correspondent Virginia Cowles really ought to be in print, available to contemporary audiences. After five decades and multiple moves (in addition to her travels she counts eleven residences in seven countries), Martha Gellhorn did not own a copy. I sent her a second-generation photocopy of the only manuscript I knew to be in existence—a blurry carbon typescript on onion-skin paper, on file at the U.S. Copyright Office at the Library of Congress. A few weeks later, in August, she replied on the back of a picture postcard of St Petersburg, "The play made me laugh out loud 3 times," and she said that she would be willing to write an introduction. *Love Goes to Press,* with an introduction by Martha Gellhorn, is published here for the first time. Gellhorn also has contributed to the publication of this book in less visible ways, answering questions, reviewing the manuscript, and sharing her only photographs of herself taken during the Second World War.

The source of the text of this edition of the play is the above-mentioned carbon typescript, registered at the Copyright Office on 11 July 1946 as *Love Goes to Press. A comedy in 3 acts.* The Copyright Office also has on record the 20 December 1945 registration of a "dramatic composition" by Gellhorn and Cowles entitled *Men Must Weep. A comedy in 3 acts,* but no manuscript is on file. On the title page of the registered manuscript, the typed title "Men Must Weep" is crossed out and replaced in Martha Gellhorn's handwriting with the title "Take My Love Away," which in turn is crossed out and replaced in an unknown hand with "Love Goes to Press."

In editing the manuscript I have made no substantive changes in the text. I have corrected obvious typographical errors and have annotated terms (such as REME: Royal Electrical and Mechanical Engineers) that are likely to be unfamiliar to today's readers. British spellings and usage (e.g., "torch" for "flashlight" and "deal table" for "card table") have been retained. Although both she and Virginia Cowles were American, Martha Gellhorn presumes that, because the play was written and originally performed in England, whoever typed the finished version would

have used British spelling. In the Afterword I summarize the play's production history, examine its critical reception in London and New York,
and offer some views about why this unusual creation—a World War II
comedy by two women war correspondents—is significant today in its
treatment of themes that are still contemporary, still contested a half
century later.

NOTE. I am most grateful for two important sources of support
for this project: a 1992 Resident Fellowship at the Oregon State
University Center for the Humanities and an Oregon State University Library Research Travel Grant.

Love Goes to Press

A Comedy in Three Acts

Cast of Characters
in order of their appearance

LEONARD LIGHTFOOT
International Information Agency

TEX CROWDER
Union Press

HANK O'REILLY
Alliance Press

JOE ROGERS
San Francisco Dispatch

MAJOR PHILIP BROOKE-JERVAUX
P.R. (Public Relations Officer)

CORPORAL CRAMP

DAPHNE RUTHERFORD, ENSA[1]

JANE MASON
New York Bulletin

ANNABELLE JONES
San Francisco World

MAJOR DICK HAWKINS, USAAF

CAPTAIN SIR ALASTAIR DRAKE
Conducting Officer

Italy, February 1944

ACT ONE
Scene
Press Camp, Poggibonsi: late afternoon.

ACT TWO
Scene One
A bedroom, Press Camp: the next morning.
Scene Two
Press Camp: early afternoon the same day.

ACT THREE
Scene
Press Camp: the following morning.

Act One
Press Camp, Poggibonsi. Late Afternoon.

This room is the converted living room of a small Italian house in the half smashed village of Poggibonsi. The walls are covered with a figured mustard coloured wallpaper. On the left is a door, leading to a covered archway and the street. In the left rear corner, there is a pile of extra army blankets, duffle bags, gas masks, etc. Someone has arranged this pile into a sort of makeshift chaise-longue. At either end of the rear wall there are windows covered with mottled upholstery curtains. Against the rear wall stands a large carved chipped ornate sideboard with a mirror panel surmounted by glassed-in shelves. One bottle decorates the shelves. There is a radio on the table part of the sideboard. A greater stretch of marked maps covers the wall alongside the sideboard and at the right extremity of the wall maps and forward at an angle, there is a deal table, with a cardboard sign saying: CAPTAIN DRAKE. *A typewriter and a field telephone and papers are arranged on the desk and a straight chair stands behind it. Towards the far end of the right wall is another door marked with a large red-lettered sign: "*PRESS ROOM. Will Correspondents kindly use." *Farther along stands a home-made bookshelf with supplies on it, paper,* PX *rations, ink, some medicines, files, etc. Close to the right front of the stage is a third door, leading into the hall and the stairway to the second floor. At the right, frontstage, there is a long rectangular table, obviously the former dining room table of this house. This is the* P.R.'*s desk and also has a field telephone, typewriter and papers on it. The far end of this table is empty and two chairs are placed at this end, and a third chair stands behind the table. To the left, downstage, there is a low army kerosene stove surrounded by a sofa with a broken spring, and of a hideous green colour, two former comfortable chairs, of antique design and in a state of great disrepair, and a small single-legged round table. Books and newspapers lie on the floor near this table.*

(*As the curtain rises,* TWO CORRESPONDENTS *are sitting at the far end of the* P.R.*'s desk, playing gin rummy.* ANOTHER JOURNALIST *is typing rather uncomfortably at the little round table. The radio is turned on, and the news is being announced in Czech.*)

LEONARD. (*patient but crabbed*) Is anyone listening?

TEX. I'm following every word. Those Czechs, I often say. Best little broadcasters in the world.

(LEONARD *rises to turn off the radio and returns to his table, but he has lost the thread of what he was writing and now sits there, silent and brooding.*)

LEONARD. It's impossible to work in this press camp.

HANK. What's the matter with our press camp?

TEX. Aside from the food and the lack of liquor and the cold and the plumbing and the transport and the telephone and the dispatch riders and the other correspondents.

HANK. Don't you like the Public Relations officers, Leonard?

LEONARD. I think Major Brooke-Jervaux is a most conscientious officer. Of course he hasn't had a great deal of experience in this branch of the service. Frankly it's the atmosphere I object to. I don't mean any offense but the correspondents here are not what I'd call really responsible journalists.

HANK. Want that card, Tex?

TEX. Yeh. Leonard, you say such cruel things. My friend Mr. O'Reilly is internationally known for being as reliable as a goat. I myself am read by millions who always refer to me as Old Reliable Crowder. Our famous colleague, Mr. Rogers, now drinking in the kitchen, is often described as a pundit. The other correspondents are young men who occasionally make mistakes.

HANK. I don't know as I'd call it mistakes. You mean the way they report a town's captured when it isn't? Hell, that's enthusiasm.

LEONARD. If you will forgive me, I will try to finish my story.

TEX. Certainly, Leonard, go right ahead.

(TEX *rises and spins the radio dial which produces the usual blare of programme selections; he leaves the radio on, playing cowboy music, fairly loud.*)

HANK. I'm glad I'm not a young man starting out in life.

TEX. Me too.

HANK. Think of our poor dumb ambitious colleagues wading around those roads near Mount Sorello.

TEX. It's their eye-witness stuff. "I rode in on the lead tank; I spear-headed the infantry; I caught the mortar shells in my teeth; I dug up the mines with my pocket knife." The silly bastards.

HANK. Stick to re-writing the communiqué and live for ever, that's my motto.

LEONARD. (*irritably*) Is anyone listening to this music?

TEX. (*noticing the music*) I'm not so much listening as bathing in beauty.

(*The telephone of the* P.R.*'s desk rings insistently. Neither of the card players move. The typing* JOURNALIST, *furiously, gets up to answer it.*)

LEONARD. No, he's not here. (*pause*) I'm sorry I'm very busy. There isn't any place to look. (*He hangs up.*) They want Captain Drake at Corps. He's supposed to take some Lend Lease[2] types to the front.

(LEONARD *turns off the radio and returns to his table.*)

HANK. They can thank their God if he doesn't show up

TEX. He only got that last M.P.[3] shot through the thigh.

(LEONARD *is typing, not listening. The* TWO MEN *play in silence.*)

HANK. Even for the Army, it's a pretty good effort to dress up Drake as a conducting officer.

TEX. You don't understand, Hank. Drake's a gent. Finest regiment in England. You know: come on chaps, up and at 'em. Follow your Captain. What does he need to read maps for?

HANK. I bet his regiment was happy when they sent him over here to kill civilians.

LEONARD. (*who has been fussing around, looking under papers on the floor*) I've lost my pipe again.

TEX. Tragic situation.

HANK. In the bathroom.

LEONARD. (*irritably, rising*) I never get a minute's peace.

(LEONARD *leaves by the hall door.*)

(*As soon as he has gone out of the room,* TEX *and* HANK *move over to his table, where* TEX *rolls up the copy paper so that he can read what* LEONARD *has been writing.*)

TEX. (*reading*) "During the first flying weather this week, C-47's of the MAAF[4] dropped parachuted supplies to the encircled American garrison on Mount Sorello. The garrison, whose fate seemed yesterday very uncertain, is now well stocked with ammunition, food and even blankets."

HANK. (*who has already moved over to* DRAKE's *table, putting paper in the machine*) Read the first sentence again.

TEX. "C-47's of the MAAF dropped parachuted supplies . . ."

HANK. That'll do. (*He types.*)

(TEX *goes to the* P.R. *table and puts paper in the machine.* JOE ROGERS *comes in from outside door, and sits down on the sofa, and picks up* Life.)

ROGERS. What's inspired you two?

TEX. Good old Leonard. We ought to give him a present sometime.

HANK. (*typing*) Don't want to spoil him, do we?

(*The Public Relations Officer,* MAJOR PHILIP BROOKE-JERVAUX, *enters from the outside door.*)

PHILIP. (*pointing to the sign over the Press Room door*) I assume you gentlemen can read. That's my typewriter, Tex.

TEX. I know, old boy. Just a minute now.

PHILIP. (*wearily*) Why don't you use the Press Room?

HANK. (*finishing his story*) Why don't you put a stove in there, you big bully?

(TEX *pulls his story out of the machine and the* P.R. *goes to sit at his own desk.* TEX *and* HANK *are standing near the stove re-reading their copy when* LEONARD *returns. He looks at them suspiciously and sits again at his typewriter.*)

(CORPORAL CRAMP *enters from the Press Room.*)

ROGERS. Good day, Cramp.

(CRAMP *smiles and goes to the* P.R.)

CRAMP. A signal, sir.

HANK. Take these to transmissions, will you, Corporal?

(*They hand him their copy and return to their card game.*)

PHILIP. (*with the signal in his hand, violently*) By God, I won't have it.

TEX. (*languidly*) Relax, Philip. It's going to be a long war.

PHILIP. Those bloody fools in Naples are sending a woman corre-spondent up here. (*Starts to take field telephone while looking at signal. Puts phone down.*) No. She'll have left. They know I won't have women. I'll put in a report on this. That Naples gang . . .

HANK. (*hopefully*) Maybe she's good-looking.

PHILIP. I don't care if she's Helen of Troy.

HANK. That's very careless talk.

PHILIP. Dressed up in Molyneux[5] uniforms. Cooing at all the men. They act as if the war was some sort of special coming-out party. Want to go to the front, and scream when they get there. Any decent woman would stay at home. There are plenty of quiet useful civilian jobs for women.

TEX. Who is this babe?

PHILIP. (*muttering*) She'll be a really nasty one. The "internationally known, glamorous war correspondent" Jane Mason.

TEX. Not Jane! Oh, goody!

HANK. We can certainly use her in this hell-hole.

PHILIP. (*disgustedly*) You're sex-starved, that's what you are.

TEX. Maybe we are, but you can't make Jane anyhow! She's not the type.

ROGERS. (*putting down his magazine lazily*) I think I'll move in with the Field Security while she's here. I'm allergic to newspaper women. I married one once. They never stop trying to scoop you, and when you scoop them they divorce you. I plan to by-pass Miss Mason.

(*Exit* ROGERS *via Press Room door.*)

TEX. (*mildly, to* HANK) Jane will love it here, won't she?

(PHILIP *has rung the bell meanwhile, and now* CORPORAL CRAMP *comes in from the outside door.*)

CRAMP. Yes, sir?

PHILIP. A lady correspondent is arriving this afternoon.

CRAMP. Yes, sir.

PHILIP. She is to have no special privileges. You understand, Cramp? No hot water, no late breakfast, no stove in her room.

CRAMP. Yes, sir. Where shall I put the lady?

PHILIP. (*to the room*) Naples wouldn't think of that. Eleven correspondents sleeping like sardines, and they throw in a woman. They ought to find a hotel-keeper for this job.

CRAMP. There's the storeroom, sir. Of course, it's not a very nice room for a lady.

PHILIP. It's nice and cold, isn't it, Cramp? You needn't bother to clean it. Just set up a cot.

CRAMP. Yes, sir.

(*exits by hall door*)

PHILIP. (*grimly*) Miss Mason won't stay long. If Drake comes in, tell him I'm in transmissions, will you, Tex?

(PHILIP *picks up papers from his desk and exits via Press Room door.*)

LEONARD. (*who is reading* Stars and Stripes[6]) Look at this.

TEX. (*not looking*) We're busy, Leonard.

LEONARD. No, listen. It's one of those gossip things you Americans go in for. It says: "Rumour has it that in a few days Daphne Rutherford, the beautiful young English actress now performing with ENSA in Naples will become the bride of our old friend Joe Rogers, the war correspondent who asks you if you come from San Francisco. It's a war-time romance, as Daphne and Joe met in London a few months ago. The G.I.'s who have been gladdening their eyes with a glimpse of Daphne will certainly wish her and Joe the best of luck."

HANK. Rogers strikes me as a close-mouthed bird, now I think of it. All of a sudden we hear he's married, then all of a sudden we hear he's divorced, and now all of a sudden we hear he's engaged.

TEX. Down for six.

HANK. I've only got two.

(HANK *marks down the score.*)

TEX. Jane must have something cooked up.

HANK. Anybody who can cook up anything in Italy is good, brother.

TEX. I never saw that girl walk a foot if she could help it. If she's taking the trouble to come to Poggibonsi, she's got something.

HANK. I haven't been on a story with Jane since Finland. Wonder where Annabelle is. It won't seem right to have Jane around without Annabelle.

TEX. God, what a pair! Do you remember Annabelle's get-up? Mink, and flannel slacks, and a hair-ribbon.

HANK. Jane wouldn't get out of bed the first week she was in Helsinki on the grounds the climate was sub-human. I don't see how she's stuck to this racket considering the way she always screamed for her comforts.

LEONARD. Do these women ever write anything?

TEX. Leonard, sometimes your ignorance shocks Mr. O'Reilly and myself. We know you try, but sometimes frankly you appall us.

LEONARD. I don't pretend to follow the American press.

HANK. Let me warn you, Leonard. Don't be deceived by Miss Mason. She and her pal Miss Jones sail around looking like *Vogue* illustrations and they get the stories before you've even heard of them. Some of our colleagues have a low opinion of those girls just because of that little trait.

TEX. You were pretty sour yourself, in Helsinki, Hank. You were still arguing about transport to the Mannerheim Line,⁷ and Jane and Annabelle were already out flying bomber missions in those old death traps. You were an angry man, as I remember.

HANK. I've forgiven them. That was a couple of wars ago.

LEONARD. They sound like rather unusual people.

TEX. They're not so much unusual as they're crazy. Specially Annabelle. Her father's a millionaire, and all she wants to do is save the world.

HANK. We ought to have a party for Jane tonight. I think I'll get off a short situationer and then we might go out and find something to drink.

TEX. Situationer on what?

HANK. I'll pick up a cross section of Italian public opinion in the kitchen.

TEX. On what?

HANK. Anything. Military government maybe.

TEX. You ought to pay that cook. He's been authoritative sources, reliable government circles, and last week by God, you quoted him as a high-ranking Allied officer.

HANK. I did not. That was my jeep driver.

TEX. We've got time for another game.

HANK. Okay. That's a pretty quick-talking cook. Your deal, isn't it?

(*They start to deal the cards, when the door on the left of the stage opens and a* GIRL *walks in. She is wearing an* ENSA *uniform, with a mink coat thrown over her shoulders. She is young with a very pretty brightly expressionless face, blue eyes and long blonde hair. She has a bright bird-like look, talks breathlessly fast, and all the time. She is 22 years old and hasn't a minute to waste.*)

DAPHNE. Oh, I'm so sorry. I've evidently come in the wrong way through the kitchen, imagine that.

(LEONARD *rises, but* TEX *and* HANK *just pause to look, mildly surprised, nod and smile, then resume their game.*)

DAPHNE. (*to* LEONARD) Oh, don't get up. I know I'm disturbing you. (*then, looking at the* CARD PLAYERS) This is the Press Camp, isn't it?

LEONARD. Yes, it is. Can I help you?

DAPHNE. Oh dear, I don't know. I'm looking for Joe Rogers. Is he staying here by any chance?

LEONARD. Why yes, he's just gone out. Let me take your coat. Won't you sit down and wait?

DAPHNE. How fortunate, thank you so much! I just arrived here this afternoon, I'm billeted in a house down the street and someone said there was a Press Camp up here and I wondered whether it was the place Joe is always talking about.

LEONARD. (*noticing* ENSA *badge*) I say, you're not Daphne Rutherford, are you?

DAPHNE. (*delighted*) But how did you know?

LEONARD. I was reading about you. Just the minute before you came in.

DAPHNE. About me? Where? In what? What does it say?

LEONARD. Here. In *Stars and Stripes*. About you and Joe Rogers. (*He shows* DAPHNE *the paper.*)

DAPHNE. (*reading*) Oh, how naughty of them! Really, they shouldn't have done that! Joe and I wanted to keep it a secret. One has to be so terribly careful with the Press, doesn't one? I don't mean your sort of Press, of course, I mean ordinary reporters.

LEONARD. I know what you mean. The American press does not have our feeling for individual privacy.

DAPHNE. (*cheerfully*) Oh well, there's no sense in worrying about it. (*walking towards sofa*) What a sweet little room. Are you war correspondents too?

(HANK *and* TEX *turn around, give her a sour smile and turn back to the game again.*)

You'll probably think it's awfully silly of me but I've never met any war correspondents before. Except Joe, of course. And I've only known him a month. We met in London. He came to a party someone gave for me and do you know when I heard his name it didn't mean a thing to me but I suppose there's no reason why it should really, since he writes for American papers, but you're English aren't you, so perhaps I've heard of you.

LEONARD. I'm Leonard Lightfoot of International Information Agency.

DAPHNE. Not really! I had a feeling I would know *you*. I read every word you write, you always make everything so clear and interesting, and I often say to myself, "How does he do it, battle after battle."

LEONARD. Oh, I don't think I do more than anyone else.

HANK. You do the work of three, Leonard. Don't be so modest.

DAPHNE. I think it's wonderful. I'm afraid I'm not very brave myself. I know it's silly, but I was even afraid to come to Italy. I wouldn't have done it if it hadn't been for Joe. But we were only starting to be engaged in England and I thought I ought to see a bit more of him . . . you know how it is . . . and it was the only way I could manage it. Of course I never expected to find myself right up here at the front. Joe will be terribly surprised when he sees me, he knows what an awful "fraidy cat" I am.

LEONARD. I think the bravest people are the ones who admit they're afraid but go right on doing their duty in spite of it.

DAPHNE. Oh, but I'm not going right on doing this. I'm only staying up here one night; in fact it's all been a dreadful mistake. When they asked me to sing to a regiment in reserve I naturally never thought it would be all the way up here at the front; they just said Poggibonsi and who in the world could be expected to know where Poggibonsi is?

(*There is a distant whistle and crash of a shell.* DAPHNE *buries her head on* LEONARD'S *shoulder.*)

DAPHNE. Heavens, what's that?

LEONARD. (*protectingly*) Only a shell. Don't be frightened. It's a long way off.

(HANK *turns around, regards the scene with distaste, and turns back to cards.*)

DAPHNE. Do you suppose this will go on all night? I'll never get through the show if it does. I know it's terrible to be so highly strung, but there isn't even a shelter at the house I'm billeted in. Goodness, I do think Joe's so right when he says war's no place for a woman. He says he's going to bundle me up and send me straight off to America where it's safe.

LEONARD. You're not giving up your career, are you?

DAPHNE. A career isn't everything, is it? I'm going to the States to stay with his mother until the war is over and have a darling little house waiting for Joe when he comes back. Where *do* you suppose he can be? My heart's still thumping away, can you hear it? I'll certainly never come up to the front again.

HANK. (*coldly*) The front is eight miles away.

DAPHNE. You mean the Germans are only eight miles away? Sometimes I have to pinch myself, what times we're living through.

TEX. Joe might be down at the Field Security. Come to think of it, he mentioned something like that.

DAPHNE. Perhaps I could find him there.

LEONARD. I'd be glad to go with you if you like. It's quicker this way. (*He directs* DAPHNE *to Press Room door.*)

DAPHNE. How kind of you. (*to* TEX *and* HANK) Well goodbye. Do come to the show tonight if you're not working.

(*as they exit via Press Room door*)
I know it's awfully silly of me, but I simply dread walking about the streets alone with all these Italians here.

HANK. Nice work, Crowder.

TEX. (*sighing*) God help Joe's poor old mother.

HANK. I don't get it. Where does Joe's poor old mother live?

TEX. Two easy guesses.

HANK. New York?

TEX. Hollywood.

HANK. (*thoughtfully*) Clever little Daphne. It could have been Ponca City.

(*Enter* CRAMP *from street door.*)

CRAMP. Everyone has gone to the briefing at Corps, sir. The Major is leaving now. He said to tell you there's no other transport, if you want to come along.

TEX. (*bitterly*) What do you think that briefing Brigadier has on his mind? I'd have this game.

HANK. (*picks up the cards*) Now I wonder where I left my mittens?

(TEX *and* HANK *exit through Press Room door.*)

(CRAMP *goes about picking up ashtrays and tidying room. The outside door opens and* JANE MASON *enters, wearily, dragging a huge suitcase, and carrying a crocodile leather make-up case. She is wet and obviously cold. She is wearing battle-dress jacket and skirt, fleece-lined galoshes, a large army overcoat with a red woollen scarf over her hair. She is small and delicate with short golden curls. She groans slightly as she hauls the suitcase over the threshold.*)

CRAMP. Let me help you with that, Miss.

(CRAMP *takes the suitcase into the room.*)

JANE. I'm Miss Mason. Would you tell the P.R. I'm here, Corporal.

CRAMP. Everyone's gone to the briefing at Corps, Miss. You're expected. Shall I show you your room?

(JANE *is beginning to unwrap and discard her gloves, coat, scarf, etc.*)

JANE. Oof.

CRAMP. You must be cold, aren't you?

JANE. I don't know. I've passed the point where I feel anything.

CRAMP. I'll get you a nice cup of tea, Miss. You'll soon warm up.

JANE. That's sweet of you, Corporal. What sort of transportation do you have up here?

CRAMP. Jeeps.

JANE. Just jeeps?

CRAMP. Yes, Miss.

JANE. I'm through with jeeps. They're torture boxes in this weather.

CRAMP. Yes, Miss. I'll fetch your tea.

(*Exit* CRAMP *via outside door.*)

(JANE *looks around the room without special interest and goes over to the field telephone on the* P.R.'s *desk.*)

JANE. Operator, give me Cyclone, please. Hello, Cyclone, put me on to Cricket, will you? What's that, Cyclone? No, I'm not a nurse. New York. Oh really, I couldn't guess. Mississippi? Alabama? Listen, Operator, while I'm concentrating on your birthplace will you get me through to Cricket? Hello, Cricket, I can scarcely hear you. 8 Corps, please. No, I'm not a nurse. Cricket? Operator, *how* did Tiger get on this line? No. 8 Corps? I want to speak to the General, please. (*louder*) The General—the Corps Commander—Sir Archibald Pinkerton. Don't cut me off. Jane Mason. Yes, he'll know. Oh, *don't* cut me off. Pinkie? What a time I've had getting you. I'm at your Corps Press Camp, and they've only got jeeps. It's too cold for jeeps, Pinkie. You couldn't be an angel and loan me a staff car for a few days, could you? Something with windows. Speak up, duckie, I can't hear you. Here at the Press Camp, only a few miles from your headquarters. How sweet of you, Pinkie. You'll send it tomorrow morning? No, I'm afraid I can't dine. I just got here. I haven't checked in with the P.R. or anything. Thanks again, darling. Goodbye.

(CRAMP *returns, bearing a thick white cup full of coal black tea. He gives it to* JANE.)

CRAMP. I'll take your luggage upstairs, Miss; call me if you want anything.

JANE. Thank you, Corporal. I'm going to thaw out here by this blazing fire. (*She goes over and sits near the small dingy kerosene stove.*)

(CRAMP *exits with luggage via hall doorway.*)

(*After a moment of silence a woman's voice is heard from outside.* JANE *is looking very sleepy and relaxed and pays no attention to the voice.*)

VOICE. This has to be the place. If it looks like a real slum it's always the Press Camp.

(*Now someone kicks open the door. It is* ANNABELLE JONES, *who is carrying a musette bag and trailing a muddy unfolded army blanket. She too is wet and cold. She is wearing battle-dress jacket and pants and boots, a huge army mackintosh, and fur gloves. She is tall and with long dark hair, curling to her shoulders. She has a vivid gay face and is 27 years old, the same age as* JANE. JANE *is sitting with her back to the door.*)

ANNABELLE. I beg your pardon. . . .

JANE. (*turns round*)

ANNABELLE. Jane!

JANE. (*rising*) Not true! What are you doing in Italy?

ANNABELL. (*dropping her possessions and running across the room to hug* JANE) I heard there was a Press Camp so I came along to see if any of the comrades were staying here. Never dreamed I'd find you in this loathsome country.

JANE. Why don't you answer letters, you great oaf. We just missed each other in Cairo last year. *What* have you been doing? Where've you come from?

ANNABELLE. Bari. Sweating to get myself to Yugoslavia. And when I had one foot in the plane the Public Relations Gang fixed me.

JANE. Those filthy P.R.'s. They seem to think they're hired to drive the Press mad.

ANNABELLE. If I'm told once more I can't do something because I'm a woman . . .

JANE. (*reciting*) What if you got wounded, Miss Jones? All the forces on land, sea and air would stop fighting the war and take care of you. Not good for the war effort.

ANNABELLE. And considering the number of times we couldn't even get out of a car when a shelling started because the men pinned us down with their elbows while they stepped over us. It makes me sick with rage. Darling, your hair's wonderful cut short like that.

JANE. Do you like it? I started it in the desert, about Alamein[8] it must have been. I couldn't get any water to wash it.

(*There is a knock on the door.*)

VOICE. (*outside*) Would you open the door? My hands are full.

ANNABELLE. (*opening door*) Poor thing. What an awful lot to carry.

UNSEEN MAN. That's okay. Made it in two trips.

(*Enter* DICK HAWKINS, *a large blond, good-looking American Air Force Officer, with his cap on the back of his head, and slightly winded. He hauls into the room a big duffle bag, and what was once an expensive, handsome, very big suitcase. These he deposits on one side of the table.*)

ANNABELLE. Jane, this is Major Hawkins. Miss Mason.

(JANE *nods.*)

Dick flew me over from Bari. He's been coping with my luggage all day. Too sweet, isn't it?

(*They both nod and smile vigorously.*)

DICK. (*to* JANE, *showing a bottle of Italian cognac*) All right with you? Annabelle was sneezing and she needs to warm up.

ANNABELLE. (*patiently*) What a splendid idea, darling. Make yourself cozy.

JANE. There must be glasses around somewhere.

(DICK *is trying to open bottle with penknife.*)

DICK. (*to* JANE) Are you a war correspondent too?

ANNABELLE. (*to* DICK) You're not the reading type, are you, Dickie? Miss Mason's on her third war.

DICK. (*heartily*) Well, I never. Honestly, you girls beat me. Here you are, two little American girls, and Annabelle wanted to fly into Yugoslavia and you go to the front and all. Why, any man would give his eyes just to take care of girls like you, and instead you go off doing these dangerous things.

(BOTH GIRLS *have been looking at him with complete loathing during this speech.*)

ANNABELLE. (*patiently*) The drinks, Dickie.

(*He struggles with the bottle while* ANNABELLE *looks at* JANE *and shrugs as if to say, "What can you do?"*)

(JANE *smiles understandingly.*)

DICK. This pocket knife won't work.

ANNABELLE. (*talking as to a poodle or a child*) Why don't you find the kitchen and borrow a bottle opener from somebody?

JANE. That way. (*She points to the outside door.*)

DICK. Sure thing. Be back in a minute.

(DICK *exits.*)

JANE. Who's that one?

ANNABELLE. I met him in Bari. He's apparently something very special in the Air Force. You know how it is.

JANE. I've never seen you without an errand brigade.

ANNABELLE. (*knocking on wood*) Imagine what it will be like when we have long grey curls and no one to carry our luggage. By the way, how's your love life?

JANE. Bad. I got slightly involved with a Frenchman in Tunis last summer, but then we invaded Sicily, and I had to leave him. It's a hopeless profession, Annabelle. There's not even time for romance. When this assignment's over I'm going to chuck my job. For good.

ANNABELLE. I don't believe it. You're always saying that.

JANE. No, really, I mean it. I *hate* this ghastly life. Everything about it. The discomfort, the red tape, the people you have to be nice to, and frankly I'm even tired of being shot at.

ANNABELLE. What else is there to do?

JANE. Millions of women do something else.

ANNABELLE. But it's so deadly.

JANE. How do we know? We've never tried.

ANNABELLE. Besides—

JANE. Besides what?

ANNABELLE. Well, we have to write, Jane. The people who fight can't. It's our job. (*hesitating*) Our duty, really.

JANE. (*smiling*) So you're still out to save the world, are you? Still looking after the human race?

ANNABELLE. Sure. That's my mother complex.

JANE. (*giggling*) I'll never forget when you turned up in Spain to battle for the under-dog in that black Schiaparelli[9] number.

ANNABELLE. At that time very few people knew how to dress for a war. What's the matter with you? You haven't got mixed up in your politics, have you?

JANE. (*laughing*) No, darling, you needn't worry about my politics. Only I don't believe we do much good. Either you can't write anything the way it really is, or else no one will believe you.

ANNABELLE. You have to go on trying.

JANE. You're better at lost causes than I am. Personally I've reached the age when there's nothing left but marriage.

ANNABELLE. (*scandalized*) That's the most defeatist statement I've ever heard.

JANE. I want a house with ten bathrooms all full of hot water, and a husband who never stops saying "Are you comfortable, my sweet?"

ANNABELLE. Husbands don't say that. Take it from me.

JANE. How do you mean? Take it from me?

ANNABELLE. I did it, of course.

JANE. You didn't! When? Where? Who is he?

ANNABELLE. In Russia, about a year and a half ago. Did you ever meet Joe Rogers anywhere?

JANE. No, but I know his name. Why didn't I hear?

ANNABELLE. Because we kept it secret. He works for the rival San Francisco paper. We didn't want our Editors to think marriage would interfere with the cut-throat competition. Not that Rogers' Editor had to worry. It turned out he married me to silence the opposition.

JANE. What are you talking about?

ANNABELLE. What would you think if your husband's first conscious act after the honeymoon was to steal your stories?

JANE. I wouldn't think. I'd steal his.

ANNABELLE. He never had any. He just waited around until I dug something up, and then he pinched it. You know how hard it is to get to the front, anywhere?

JANE. Really, Annabelle, what a question.

ANNABELLE. Well, it's just twenty times harder in Russia. And I had it all laid on. Rogers stole that trip too.

JANE. I must say that's unforgivable.

ANNABELLE. Certainly it's unforgivable. He said he did it because he loved me so much he couldn't bear to have me in danger.

JANE. If he said he did it because he had scarlet fever or because his mother was ill or anything like that, you'd have forgiven him.

ANNABELLE. I did anyway. But my Editor ordered me home. I couldn't blame the old goof, either. Of course Rogers' Editor didn't order him home, he offered him a vacation. When we got back to San Francisco, Rogers' Editor gave him a bonus and my Editor said, "Annabelle, we think perhaps you're a little tired. Take a rest, my child, and then try the South Pacific and kindly don't get scooped by the *Dispatch* from here to Japan."

JANE. I didn't know you'd been in the South Pacific.

ANNABELLE. I only got as far as Mexico. That was our second honeymoon. Then Rogers did it again.

JANE. Did what, chum?

ANNABELLE. There was a classy international murder in one of the villas and I got the story as usual. Rogers popped back from a day's fishing and said he'd file it for me. I was supposedly too tired. So he sent it the slowest rate he could find and wrote himself a fine piece and telephoned it through.

(*Dick enters without knocking.*)

DICK. (*jovially*) We had to push the cork in finally.

(*The girls pay no attention.*)

ANNABELLE. After that I bought a twenty-four hour divorce in Mexico City, and wired Rogers the news, and took a plane to New York.

DICK. You poor kid. What did he do to you? Go off with some dame? I'd like to beat the hell out of him.

ANNABELLE. (*with dignity*) My former husband was as faithful as a collie.

DICK. Probably drunk all the time. The dirty rat. What sort of a way to treat a sweet little girl? It's a tough story I mean. We need some glasses.

JANE. That way. (*pointing to outside door*)

DICK. Be back in a minute.

ANNABELLE. Bring some water too, darling. That cognac's not drinkable straight.

(*Exit* DICK.)

JANE. Why did you fall in love with Mr. Rogers in the first place?

ANNABELLE. You can't tell from the outside that he's got the character of a cobra. From the outside he's a beautiful, funny, fascinating man.

JANE. (*anxious at the way* ANNABELLE *has said it*) You're not still a little in love with this beautiful, funny, fascinating man, are you?

ANNABELLE. I haven't seen him for eight months. He's probably riding around on an aircraft-carrier in the Coral Sea.

JANE. That's no answer, Annabelle.

(*Enter* DICK *without knocking*)

DICK. (*Pouring drink. To* JANE) How much?

JANE. An inch or two. (*looking at* ANNABELLE) I think you are, you know.

(*The phone rings before* ANNABELLE *can answer.* ANNABELLE *gets up and collects her drink and takes off more of her outer clothing.* DICK *mixes drinks. It is seen that he is drinking straight cognac.*)

JANE. Hello. This is Jane Mason. Oh Steve! (*pause*) Yes, just arrived fifteen minutes ago. How marvelous! You've got the number. . . . And don't tell anyone, Steve. You're a wonder. Goodbye.

ANNABELLE. (*drinking*) What's that about?

JANE. Only a story.

ANNABELLE. (*sternly*) Now, Jane.

JANE. (*looking at both of them*) It's top secret.

DICK. You two girls certainly tickle me.

ANNABELLE. Dick, please!

JANE. You know the American garrison that's cut off up here on Mount Sorello?

ANNABELLE. Everybody knows.

JANE. (*nodding*) If they can hold out a few more days, there'll be an attack through this front to relieve them.

ANNABELLE. I don't see how they've hung on this long.

JANE. Well, that's it. That's my story.

ANNABELLE. (*disappointed*) Of course you can't write too much about them, but it's been front page news for almost a week, hasn't it?

JANE. Oh I'm not doing that. I'm going up to the garrison before the attack and stay until they're relieved.

ANNABELLE. How can you? You can't get through the Germans and you can't land a plane on a mountain.

JANE. That's what the telephone call was about. The Germans agreed to let ambulances through to evacuate wounded. I'm civilian personnel so it's okay for me to go along.

DICK. But the krauts are blowing that place off the map. They must be crazy to take a girl like you. . . .

ANNABELLE. Dick, please! Jane, it's too beautiful. No-one's ever got a story that way. Why will the Germans play?

JANE. Because we'll bring back an equal number of their wounded.

DICK. I can't get over you girls.

ANNABELLE. When are you going?

JANE. Tomorrow. Steve'll send for me here.

ANNABELLE. If the P.R. knows he'll stop you.

JANE. (*firmly*) The P.R. will hear about this when it's over.

ANNABELLE. It's a beauty, Jane. (*to* DICK) The difference between my colleague, Miss Mason, and myself is that she gets where she's going.

JANE. Really, Annabelle! I've never been torpedoed. How about the stories you did after you got sunk on that English Destroyer? And those Maginot Line[10] stories? *Nobody* was there.

ANNABELLE. I used to get places. But not any more.

DICK. (*comfortingly*) That Yugoslav trip is a rugged deal, Annabelle. Those planes crack up all the time.

ANNABELLE. I wasn't going for the ride, Dickie. I *like* those Yugs. I'm on their side. Look, let's never talk about it again, shall we?

DICK. (*putting his arm around* ANNABELLE'*s shoulder*) It's a shame the way people've been treating you. You're one of the sweetest little girls I ever met and it's not right, that's all. I'm going to take you to Poland.

JANE *and* ANNABELLE. (*both sitting up absolutely straight*) You're WHAT?

DICK. (*obstinately*) Yes I am, and that's a better story than Yugoslavia. I've done 'em both, and it's a damn sight harder flight too. I'm in command of my ship and the squadron as far as that goes and I can do what I want. And by God I'm going to take you.

ANNABELLE. (*breathlessly*) When?

DICK. (*getting careful*) Now listen, if you say anything about this there'll be hell to pay. Security. And I won't tell you when nor where from nor whereabouts in Poland we're going, see? Because that's my business. I just tell you I'll take you and soon. I'm going to Caserta now to get some more gen on this trip.

JANE. (*respectfully*) Do you do it often?

DICK. We do it, and the English do it. Sometimes we drop them stuff by parachute. And sometimes we land and pick up people that they got to get out of the country. That's what we're doing this time. Now, Annabelle, does that make it all right about Yugoslavia?

ANNABELLE. Oh darling, more than all right. But what do I do? I mean is it a question of days, or a week or what?

DICK. I don't know yet, but it's soon.

JANE. Why couldn't you wait here with me?

DICK. That's okay. I can telephone you or send my jeep.

JANE. And if you need any transport while you're waiting, I'll give you mine.

ANNABELLE. You mean to say you've got a jeep of your own?

JANE. Not at all. A big closed staff car—thanks to Pinkie, a lovely General I met during the retreat in France.

ANNABELLE. Not Archie Pinkie?

JANE. Yes. . . .

ANNABELLE. But I met him during the retreat in Greece! He's Heaven.

JANE. Isn't he? I lost track of him for nearly two years, and then I saw him again in North Africa during the retreat at Kasserine.

DICK. Say, who is this Pinkie?

ANNABELLE. Someone almost as angelic as you are, darling.

(*She kisses him on the top of the head.*)

DICK. You better stick pretty close, Annabelle, because when we get the word we move. I ought to be shoving now. See you girls soon.

ANNABELLE. (*fiercely*) If anyone tries to stop this trip . . .

DICK. (*pats her head gaily*) I'll beat the hell out of him.

> (*Exit* DICK *via Press Room door, waving to them both.*)

ANNABELLE. Oh Jane, isn't it lovely to be at the same war again!

(HANK *and* TEX *enter from the outside door, blowing their noses and slapping their hands together. The girls get up as they enter.*)

JANE. You two! Oh bliss!

TEX. Papa's baby. God, how you'll brighten this dump.

(*He hugs* JANE, *lifting her up in his arms.*)

(*To* ANNABELLE) Hello, you great black-eyed beauty. We didn't expect you. This gets better all the time.

HANK. My Annabelle! You're prettier every war.

ANNABELLE. (*kissing him*) Hello, goof! (*kissing* TEX) Hello, darling. You look wonderful.

TEX. I look as fat as a pig unless you're blind.

JANE. Hank, take off some clothes so we can see you. It's no use masquerading as a buffalo.

ANNABELLE. Sweet little place you've got here.

TEX. Yes, isn't it? Elsie de Wolfe[11] whipped it up for us a few weeks ago.

JANE. Nice and cold too.

TEX. Cold nothing. This is where we grow our orchids. You ought to see the Press Room.

JANE. Lots of stories?

HANK. Not a damn thing. Except Mount Sorello. And what can we do about that?

TEX. What are you looking for?

ANNABELLE. (*quickly*) Oh the usual. Local colour. Who else is here?

TEX. No-one you know. Sports writers. Out all day at the front. Heroic young men. We see to it that they stay in the Press Room. They work so much it makes us nervous.

JANE. What's the P.R. like?

HANK. You'll love him. You're made for each other. When he got your signal he made a speech about women with guts who did their own job in the world. He's turning the place over to you.

JANE. (*pleased*) He must be a remarkable P.R.

HANK. He is. A little on the wolf side. It's a pity, but he can't help it.

(*A shell lands nearer and louder. No-one notices. They wait for noise to subside.*)

JANE. Make more sense, dear.

HANK. Well, you know how women long for tall dark handsome citizens covered with D.S.O.'s.[12]

ANNABELLE. Why the D.S.O.?

TEX. Tanks. Something at Alamein. Naturally we never asked him.
He's English.

JANE. If he's so wonderful, why did he leave the Tanks? No sensible
man would be Public Relations Officer.

TEX. He's got a new sterling silver joint somewhere. Not that he
makes anything of it.

JANE. (*touched*) Oh poor thing. That's not good, is it?

(*Enter* CRAMP *from outside with tea-tray.*)

CRAMP. I brought some biscuits in case you're hungry, Miss. My wife
sent them to me. And some fresh tea for the other lady.

JANE. You're too sweet. We mustn't eat up your presents.

CRAMP. I've got plenty, Miss. (*to* ANNABELLE) Are you feeling
warmer, Miss?

ANNABELLE. Much better.

CRAMP. I'm heating some water now if you want a wash up before
supper.

JANE. You mustn't take too much trouble about us, Corporal.

CRAMP. Oh no, Miss, it's a pleasure to see some ladies who speak
English. Anything you want, you just tell me.

(PHILIP *has entered unnoticed, by Press Room door, and is listening.*)

JANE. Thank you so much.

(CRAMP *sees* PHILIP.)

CRAMP. If that's all . . .

(*They all see* PHILIP.)

TEX. Philip, come and meet the girls. Our P.R., Major Brooke-
Jervaux. Miss Mason. Miss Jones.

JANE. (*rising to shake hands*) How do you do?

PHILIP. How do you do? (*Shakes hands with* ANNABELLE.) How do
you do? You weren't mentioned in the signal from Naples, Miss Jones.

ANNABELLE. I haven't been to Naples. I landed at a field near here
and I just dropped in to see if there were any friends around.

PHILIP. You realize you're not allowed to come to this front without
permission?

JANE. As you've already accepted me, it wouldn't seem to make
much difference.

PHILIIP. (*very stuffy*) War isn't run on a basis of whims, Miss
Mason. (*to* ANNABELLE) Are your credentials in order?

JANE. Do you think she's come for the winter tourist season?

ANNABELLE. (*icily*) Would you like to see my AGO card?[13]

PHILIP. (*equally icy*) I'll have to notify Naples. Perhaps you don't
understand, Miss Jones, that we also plan in advance for our mess.

TEX. (*to* ANNABELLE) It's complicated, pal. They have to figure out
how many cans of meat and beans per day.

PHILIP. (*ignoring him*) And there is also the question of rooms.

ANNABELLE. I wouldn't dream of troubling you, Major. I'll be quite happy rolled up in a blanket anywhere.

JANE. (*airily*) The floor, the gutter, just anywhere.

ANNABELLE. You see I'm only spending one night.

PHILIP. Your return transport will be laid on for tomorrow, and meantime I suppose we could put a cot in Miss Mason's room.

JANE. (*furious*) What a talent for organization.

PHILIP. (*to* JANE) I'll ask Corporal Cramp to show you your quarters.

JANE. Don't bother. If you'll tell me where it is I'm sure I can find it. This isn't exactly Versailles.

PHILIP. That door. Upstairs to the left. The door's open.

JANE. Miss Jones would probably like her luggage, but I suppose that's a terrible imposition. Never mind. Annabelle and I are frightfully good at carrying duffle bags on our heads.

PHILIP. (*with dignity*) I'll tell Cramp. Dinner is from seven to eight.

JANE. (*bitterly*) Too kind of you.

(JANE *exits by hall door*, PHILIP *exits by outside door.*)

ANNABELLE. (*sitting in chair by stove, drinking tea*) You're a nice pair of comrades. Oh my, if I had to spend three days with the handsome Major I'd kick his teeth in.

TEX. He may already have that impression. Jane wasn't exactly patting his head.

HANK. He's not a bad chap really.

ANNABELLE. You mean those were his party manners?

HANK. You've got to be more tolerant, Annabelle. The poor guy's been away from England for three years, fighting to protect womankind from the horrors of war. And then the womankind walks in on him. He might as well have spared himself the trouble. You can see it would upset him for a while.

ANNABELLE. If there's anything I really loathe, it's a woman protector.

(CRAMP *comes in and picks up* ANNABELLE's *luggage. He passes across the stage from the outside door to the hall door.*)

CRAMP. It's five to six, sir. The other gentlemen have gone.

HANK. The communiqué again.

TEX. Work, work, work. It's the steady grind that kills you. See you later, Annabelle.

(*Exit* TEX *and* HANK *via outside door.*)

(ANNABELLE *stretches and makes herself comfortable in the chair. She is smoking and looking lazy and half asleep when the Press Room door opens.* JOE ROGERS *enters, but is talking over his shoulder to someone outside. When* ANNABELLE *sees him she sits up straight.*)

ROGERS. (*talking out into the hall*) I'm not going. It's not worth it.
(ROGERS *turns and sees* ANNABELLE *and stops dead. They stare at each other.*)

ANNABELLE. Why aren't you in the South Pacific?

ROGERS. Why should I be?

ANNABELLE. You said you were.

ROGERS. That was eight months ago. In eight months I could have been in the South Pacific, the Far West, the Near East, the Middle East, and Kansas City if I felt like it.

ANNABELLE. I trust you had a lovely time.

ROGERS. Delightful. As soon as I recovered from that telegram.

ANNABELLE. Telegrams are appalling aren't they? I used to wince every time my Editor sent me one.

ROGERS. If you're referring to that lousy Mexican murder story . . .

ANNABELLE. What an odd idea.

ROGERS. I suppose I'm responsible for the inefficiency of all cable companies, including every delay. . . .

ANNABELLE. Were there any delays? I thought your story got through quite nicely. All over the front page, as I remember.

ROGERS. Listen Annabelle, could I help it if the office happened to call in when I was trying to file my story? No-one could get any out-going calls. It was plain luck.

ANNABELLE. You *are* a lucky boy, aren't you? Remember that trip to the front in Russia? What a piece of luck that was.

ROGERS. That was different, Annabelle, and you know it. I admit I stole your trip. But what man who loved a woman wouldn't have? How could I sit in Moscow and allow my wife to be smashed into a bloody pulp, probably . . .

ANNABELLE. You said "burned alive" at the time. I can't think why.

ROGERS. Your nose is shiny.

ANNABELLE. (*composure shaken, and reaching for her handbag*) I couldn't care less.

ROGERS. Where did you get that lipstick? It looks purple.

ANNABELLE. (*angrily*) *Stop* criticizing me.

ROGERS. (*delighted*) Otherwise you're prettier than ever. Even prettier than the first time I saw you, walking into Molotov's cocktail party[14] in that red dress.

ANNABELLE. Black dress.

ROGERS. No. Red dress. And then I saw you looking at me and as soon as you could manage it you sort of sidled up to me.

ANNABELLE. I sidled up to you! I was doing very well with that Hero of the Soviet Union until you fastened yourself on me.

ROGERS. Don't get me wrong. I didn't mind. I had my eye on that red dress from the minute you came in.

ANNABELLE. Black dress.

ROGERS. But you were the most beautiful of all in Mexico. I remember the first night in Acapulco when I was waiting for you in the bar and you came down in a white evening dress and the diamonds Daddy gave you if you'd only leave me.

ANNABELLE. He did not. He gave them to me for my birthday.

ROGERS. I thought for a minute you still had on your nightgown and I was getting ready to fight every man in the bar.

ANNABELLE. You repel me.

ROGERS. You left a white satin nightgown in the bathroom. Drenched in perfume furthermore. Did you do it on purpose?

ANNABELLE. You know very well I always lose things.

ROGERS. I sat around and looked at it and smelled it until it just about drove me crazy.

ANNABELLE. You should have given it to the maid.

ROGERS. I still have it, in case you need one. I've carried it with me all the time. Of course this is all probably very distasteful to you. You wouldn't remember our balcony would you, or the wonderful place we always went swimming alone?

ANNABELLE. Acapulco is a charming resort, isn't it?

ROGERS. You've no idea how lonely a man can be, Annabelle. I went out to New Guinea. There's nothing to do but sweat in the jungle and wait for those little yellow men to snipe at you day and night. I used to think about you and wonder what you were doing.

ANNABELLE. (*moved*) It must be ghastly out there.

ROGERS. Oh it wasn't so bad for me. Not being married it didn't really matter whether I got bumped off or not; but for the men with wives—well it isn't too good. They'd show me their letters from home, and it's funny but when a man hasn't any letters of his own he gets sort of a pleasure reading other people's. When I got malaria, I used to think I still had someone. . . .

ANNABELLE. (*stricken*) Did you have malaria? Oh Joe, how awful.

ROGERS. It wasn't serious. Everyone gets malaria, but the nurses were pretty sick of the way I raved about my wife and accused them of stealing my letters.

ANNABELLE. Were you in the hospital long, Joe?

ROGERS. Only eight weeks. It was nothing, really it wasn't. And I don't blame you for what you did, darling. I know what your job means to you and what a bore it must have been with a husband always hanging around.

ANNABELLE. (*huskily*) You were never a bore. . . .

ROGERS. And how could anyone expect a girl like you with hundreds of men chasing after her to miss someone like me.

ANNABELLE. But I did miss you, Joe. There hasn't been anyone else.

ROGERS. I'm a fool to be so sentimental. It's just that being so damn lonely . . .

(*Enter* DAPHNE *and* LEONARD.)

DAPHNE. If he doesn't come soon I won't be able to wait much longer. The show begins at seven.

(JOE *and* ANNABELLE *look up;* JOE *is stunned.*)

(*to* JOE) Joe! Where have you been? I've been looking all over the place for you. (*She runs up to him, sees* ANNABELLE.) Oh I hope I'm not interrupting your work.

ROGERS. Daphne! What are you doing up here?

DAPHNE. I told Leonard you'd be surprised. I'm surprised myself. When they asked me to sing to a regiment in reserve at Poggibonsi I naturally didn't think it was going to be right up here at the front. My name is Daphne Rutherford. Joe is so bad at introducing people, isn't he? I suppose all journalists have that casual way about them.

ROGERS. Miss Annabelle Jones.

LEONARD. (*resenting being left out*) I'm Leonard Lightfoot of International Information Agency.

DAPHNE. Oh Joe, it's too dreadful, our secret's out. Some reporter has written about it in the *Stars and Stripes*. (*reaching for paper*)

ROGERS. (*hastily*) Where are you staying, Daphne?

DAPHNE. Look darling, here it is. "Rumour has it that in a few days the beautiful young English actress, silly of them isn't it, Miss Daphne Rutherford (*mumbles*) (*clear again*), will become the bride of our old friend Joe Rogers. . . ."

(*There is a silence.*)

ANNABELLE. (*quietly*) Congratulations. You shouldn't have wasted so much time gossiping about the old days, Joe, when you had much more important things to talk about.

(*Enter* JANE.)

JANE. The room's repulsive, but Corporal Cramp is a lamb. He's brought buckets of hot water.

ANNABELLE. I'm just going up. Jane, this is Mr. Rogers of the *San Francisco Dispatch* and his fiancée Miss Rutherford. Miss Mason. I'll see you upstairs.

(*Exit* ANNABELLE *via hall door.*)

JANE. Oh, how do you do?

LEONARD. I'm Leonard Lightfoot of International Information Agency.

DAPHNE. I must be going now or I'll be late for my show. You'll take me home won't you, Joe? I know it's silly, but I hate walking round the streets alone with all these Italians here. Goodbye, Miss Mason.

LEONARD. You'll need a torch, Miss Rutherford. I'll get you mine. (*as he goes through door leading to Press Room*) Meet you in front.

(*Exit* ROGERS *and* DAPHNE *through outside door, and* LEONARD *via Press Room door.*)

(JANE *moves over to wall maps and studies them.*)

(PHILIP *enters from Press Room door; he stands watching* JANE.)

PHILIP. Are you planning the next attack, Miss Mason?

JANE. (*crossly*) I resigned from the General Staff last week. Didn't you know? I was just looking at this miserable front.

PHILIP. You don't approve of the front?

JANE. I shouldn't think anyone in his right mind would approve of fighting a war up a string of mountains.

PHILIP. You probably have many valuable ideas on how to run this campaign. It's wonderfully easy to criticize, isn't it?

JANE. It would be a very good thing if we were allowed to criticize.

PHILIP. I daresay your readers find you the most brilliant military mind since Clausewitz.[15]

JANE. I daresay they do.

PHILIP. There *is* a Press Room for correspondents, Miss Mason.

JANE. From what I hear it's full of frozen corpses. Now if you would consider moving the stove . . .

PHILIP. The stove happens to be my personal property. It belonged to me in Tunisia.

JANE. I was in Tunisia. What regiment were you in?

PHILIP. (*abruptly*) The 17th Lancers. Would you forgive me if I got on with my work?

JANE. (*lightly*) Not at all. (*She stands regarding the map for a few seconds.*) Were you in the newspaper business before the war?

(PHILIP *doesn't answer but goes on writing.* JANE *looks at him and repeats slowly, deliberately, maddening.*)

Were you in the newspaper business before the war?

PHILIP. Before the war I was a farmer. I had no contact with the press and after the war I hope to have no contact with the press again. (*trying to write*) Would you *mind* . . .

JANE. Oh not at all. (*Pause.* JANE *lights a cigarette.*) Think what fun it will be when the war is over and you can hustle back to your nice old cows. . . .

PHILIP. (*furious, throwing down pen and rising*) Has anyone ever told you you're a blasted nuisance?

JANE. (*sweetly*) Not anyone with a medal for gallantry.

PHILIP. Do you mind using the Press Room, Miss Mason?

JANE. (*rising*) Not at all, Major. (*Walking towards door*) Oh dear, what a pity it all is. (*stops and looks at* PHILIP) Tall, good-looking . . . *very* good-looking . . . but *so* cross.

(*Exit* JANE *through Press Room door.*)

(PHILIP *continues his work. Enter* CAPTAIN SIR ALASTAIR DRAKE

through side door. He is about thirty years old, dressed in British uni-
form, on the plump side, with a silky Guards moustache. He exudes
wealth, health, and confidence.)

DRAKE. Hello, Philip.

PHILIP. (*crossly*) Where the hell have you been? Corps rang up six
times.

DRAKE. Awful muck-up. I forgot those Lend Lease chaps, actually.
Had rather a hard day showing that Australian correspondent round.
Took the wrong turn and it was fairly sticky for a bit. No need for the
chap to be so windy though. I'll push off now if you don't need me.
Everything O.K.?

PHILIP. No it's not. It couldn't be worse.

DRAKE. What's up, old boy?

PHILIP. Women war correspondents. Two of them. Staying here.

DRAKE. Oh I say, rather a nice change isn't it?

PHILIP. It's the end, that's all. The Jones woman doesn't matter.

DRAKE. Annabelle?

PHILIP. Yes.

DRAKE. Charming girl. Met her in Paris in '40.

PHILIP. She's leaving tomorrow so she doesn't count. But the other!
The most conceited, spoiled, bad-tempered . . . God, I wish I knew how
to get rid of her.

(PHILIP *goes on looking through papers.* DRAKE *lights a cigarette,*
thinking.)

DRAKE. You leave it to me, Philip. I've got a plan.

PHILIP. What sort of plan?

DRAKE. Nothing complicated. I'll take her on a little trip tomorrow.
She'll be delighted to leave. First excuse. Off like a shot.

PHILIP. You can't take her too near the front. There'd be a first class
flap if anything happened.

DRAKE. Of course not. I'll tell her the Pictorial boys want her picture
talking to the troops, troops all mad to see her, you know, that sort of
thing. That'll get her. Then something will crack up in the jeep and we'll
have a long healthy walk home. What's her name?

PHILIP. Jane Mason. Ever met her?

DRAKE. No, what is she? The big-footed beefy kind?

PHILIP. Certainly not. She's small and slender with blue eyes and
lovely gold hair. . . .

DRAKE. Look here, old boy, are you certain you want to get rid of
her?

PHILIP. (*with dignity*) You attend to it, Alastair. You'll meet her at
dinner.

DRAKE. As a matter of fact I'm going over to see old Chunky at the
Hamshires tonight, but I'll pick her up tomorrow morning about ten.

Don't worry about it any more. I'll take a bet she leaves for Naples in the afternoon.

PHILIP. Say hello to Chunky. If you could find some whisky . . .

DRAKE. Not a hope. Is there any work?

PHILIP. No, they're all filing equally dreary stories about Mount Sorello. The dispatch rider got lost this morning and delivered their stuff to Naples two hours late, and there's a transmission delay from Naples as well, so they're even bloodier than usual. But there's nothing to do here.

DRAKE. Well then, good night. Have a nice time with the small slender golden-haired horror.

(*Exit* DRAKE.)

(PHILIP *seems rather flustered. Then he rises, with a shy self-conscious expression, and walks across the room to the mirror on the sideboard. He has to stoop to see himself, and he stands in front of the mirror, straightening his tie.*)

CURTAIN

Act Two

Scene One. [A bedroom, Press Camp: the next morning.]

This is the former storeroom of the Press Camp, and there are wooden packing-cases in the corners, old helmets, gas masks, piles of blankets, etc., pushed out of the way against the walls. The door leading to the hall is at the centre right. There is a small shuttered window at the rear left of the stage. Alongside it, against the rear wall is a cot. Near it, on one of the packing-cases there is a candle stub and remnants of female clothing and make-up. Against the loft wall there is another cot with a small packing-case as a bedside table and on it a kerosene lamp. A round army stove stands approximately midway between the cots. The girls have scattered their clothes and possessions at random over the heaps of junk that clutter the room.

(*When the curtain rises the room is dark but the audience can see two mounds in the cots. There is a knock at the door. No answer. The knock is repeated.*)

JANE. *No!*

(CORPORAL CRAMP *enters.*)

CRAMP. I'm sorry to wake you, Miss, but General Pinkerton is on the phone.

JANE. (*from under bedcovers*) What?

CRAMP. General Pinkerton, Miss. He wants to speak to either you or Miss Jones.

JANE. Annabelle, it's Pinkie. He called last night. He wants us to dine.

ANNABELLE. (*muffled*) What's he mean ringing up in the middle of the night?

JANE. Tell him we'll phone later, will you, Corporal?

CRAMP. Certainly, Miss. Shall I bring you some tea and toast?

JANE. That *would* be nice. Is it time for breakfast?

CRAMP. Ten o'clock, Miss.

(*He exits.*)

(*There is complete silence for a few seconds.*)

JANE. (*throwing off covers*) Ten o'clock? I'm ruined!

(*She springs out of bed and is revealed wearing a battle jacket and a shirt with long shirttails, a pair of silk stockings and very frilly step-ins. She stumbles towards the window, knocking against a packing-case.*)

JANE. Oh! This torture chamber. Where's the window?

(*She finds the window and opens the shutters. There is now a gray light.*)

JANE. (*putting on army mackintosh*) I'll never be ready. *Oh,* the cold! (*searching for toothbrush*) Steve came over last night. I was so afraid someone would see him and catch on, I made him talk outside in the pouring rain. Where *is* my toothbrush? They should have thrown a hand-grenade in this room to make it really cozy.

(JANE *exits with washing equipment. Her voice is heard in the hallway following a series of impatient knocks, saying: "Hurry."*)

(ANNABELLE *slowly sits up, rubbing her back.* JANE *returns.*)

JANE. Leonard's in there. Thinking.

ANNABELLE. My back's broken. Oh, the cold! God! I think my feet are gone, too.

JANE. You're the one who loves this life. (*She begins to cold-cream her face.*)

ANNABELLE. Where *can* that draft come from? They don't have to be so mean about it. They don't have to exaggerate.

JANE. It's always like this. Even when they try to be nice, it isn't much better. You can visit me in my lovely warm house when your health fails.

ANNABELLE. That's very decent of you. I can't move.

JANE. (*combing hair and putting on make-up*) If Cramp doesn't hurry, Steve will be here before I get any tea.

ANNABELLE. Who's Steve?

JANE. (*surprised*) The Ambulance man—the one who's taking me up to the garrison. We're leaving this morning.

ANNABELLE. (*Sitting up with great interest*) No! Why didn't you tell me?

JANE. I've been telling you. He came last night and said to be ready from ten on. He's furious because they wasted four days negotiating and now the Germans say we can only send one ambulance. They realize we haven't more than three or four German wounded to bring out, and naturally they don't care about ours.

ANNABELLE. (*indignantly*) Are we going to take that?

JANE. What else can we do? It's better to save a few men.

ANNABELLE. I'm not crazy about this trip, Jane.

JANE. They're sure to be well dug in by this time. I'll probably sit in a cellar and play cards. Anyway we ought to be out of there by tomorrow night. Steve says the attack to relieve us will start at first light.

ANNABELLE. And what if the attack fails?

JANE. No sense brooding in advance, is there? That wretched Leonard ought to be clean as a pin by now.

(JANE *exits again.*)

(ANNABELLE *reaches for cold-cream and mirror;* JANE *returns almost at once.*)

JANE. Now it's Tex. I don't think that human chain will ever break.

ANNABELLE. Throw me the Kleenex, will you?

(CRAMP *enters with breakfast tray.*)

CRAMP. I hope this will do, Miss. I got the cook to make some hot buttered toast and there's some marmalade, too.

JANE. How wonderful. I can't think what we'd do without you. Give Miss Jones the tray. I'll manage over here.

(*She sits on the edge of the cot and uses the packing-case as a table.*)

CRAMP. (*pleased*) I'll put some kettles of hot water in the bathroom. If you don't mind, don't mention it to the Major.

ANNABELLE. I'm not speaking to the Major if I can help it.

CRAMP. He said to tell you your transport for Naples will be here at two o'clock, Miss Jones.

ANNABELLE. (*furiously*) I will *not* be pushed around by that man. He's too mean.

CRAMP. He's not really unkind, Miss. His bark is worse than his bite.

JANE. Have you been with him all through the war?

CRAMP. I've been with the Major's family for more than fifteen years. In peacetime I'm Mr. Philip's groom and second horseman.

ANNABELLE. It's not right for a man to like horses and hate women.

CRAMP. Oh you're wrong, Miss. Major Philip likes the ladies very much. He's just a bit conservative, so to speak. He's not used to seeing ladies on their own.

JANE. What's his wife like?

CRAMP. He's not married, Miss. Though we've seen plenty of ladies after him. I think that's what it is. Major Philip likes to make up his own mind.

(*Exit* CRAMP.)

ANNABELLE. Make up his own mind indeed! He's the nastiest bully I ever met.

JANE. He might be all right if you know how to handle him. He's very good-looking.

ANNABELLE. If you fall for that man . . .

JANE. (*hastily*) I just thought it would be fun to flirt with him a little if one had time.

ANNABELLE. (*bitterly*) My idea about men is avoid them. Hold the bums off is my theory.

JANE. I knew there was something I wanted to ask you! What about Joe? I couldn't think of anything to say when you introduced me to him—and the girl friend. He's not serious about marrying *her,* is he?

ANNABELLE. So it would seem.

JANE. (*surprised*) But darling, when you didn't show up in the Press Room I thought of course Joe had come back and you'd gone off with him somewhere. I suppose Miss Rutherford dragged him to her show.

ANNABELLE. I don't know. Leonard cornered me and when Joe hadn't come in by ten I went to bed.

JANE. He must have been stunned when he saw you. I hope he was nice.

ANNABELLE. Oh, very nice. It's so easy for him. Four sentences and I'm in the wrong. Four more sentences and I apologize. Four more and he breaks my heart. And afterwards he doesn't bother to say good night.

JANE. (*incensed*) The poor little abandoned wife. All we need now is a few yards of sackcloth, some ashes, and a comfortable wailing wall.

ANNABELLE. (*incensed too*) What I like about you is your big warm understanding heart.

JANE. I'm ashamed of you, Annabelle. Do you mean to say you're going to sit around looking pitiful and let that repugnant joke woman get Joe?

ANNABELLE. She's repugnant all right but we're not men. Remember? They see things in an odd little way of their own.

JANE. If you weren't shapeless with self-pity and would make some effort to fix yourself up, no man—not even Joe Rogers—would look at Daphne.

ANNABELLE. You're a fine loyal friend.

JANE. I am not.

ANNABELLE. Do you suppose he loves her mind? Or would it be her soul?

JANE. You know as much about men as I do. They're a set of people who are constantly mixed up about sex. They don't know what they're doing half the time.

ANNABELLE. Well, there it is.

JANE. If you can't be a little energetic about sex yourself, I can only say I'm disappointed.

ANNABELLE. What do you want me to do? Slink into his room wearing my glamorous long underwear and win him away from her?

JANE. Oh, for God's sake.

ANNABELLE. There isn't time, Jane. They're being married in three days.

JANE. What do you want? A whole week?

ANNABELLE. She tails him like the F.B.I.

JANE. She's leaving for Naples this morning.

ANNABELLE. And I'm leaving for Naples this afternoon. The Major and his transport.

JANE. Tell the Major you have a pain. Really, Annabelle. I've never listened to such spineless conversation.

ANNABELLE. Do you think I could do it?

JANE. Don't be pathetic with me.

ANNABELLE. Do you know, I think I will.

JANE. Well, *finally.*

ANNABELLE. Cleopatra Jones. Somewhat hampered by all this seductive khaki suiting.

JANE. You could shed the camel's hair undies before you start this campaign.

ANNABELLE. Yes dear. Anything else?

JANE. Not a thing. Mother has faith in you.

ANNABELLE. After I get him back, I would like to hit him on the head with a bottle. Look at all the trouble he's caused me. Still, I must say it will be quite a pleasure to have him back.

JANE. It's nice to see you acting normal again.

(*There is a knock, and* MAJOR HAWKINS *enters.*)

DICK. Buon Giorno, as we say in Italy.

ANNABELLE. Dick! How'd you get here?

JANE. How lovely! Find a nice soft packing-case and make yourself at home. Had breakfast?

DICK. (*looking around the room*) Thanks. Say, what sort of a joint is this, anyway?

ANNABELLE. Comrade, the little women are lucky not to be sleeping on the pavement. . . . What's the news?

DICK. (*cheerfully*) Nothing, except you're going to climb out of that cot.

ANNABELLE. (*tearfully*) Why?

DICK. Everything's set. We're off.

ANNABELLE. (*faltering*) Right now?

DICK. As soon as my jeep's fixed. I thought I'd call for you myself, I didn't want to shout it around the squadron that you were coming with us. The jeep's conked out, but the fellows at the REME[16] say they'll have it going in twenty minutes. Think you can make it by then?

ANNABELLE. Twenty minutes? Oh Dickie, how awful!

DICK. Well, I can wait half an hour, honey, don't get upset. It's only that I've got a lot to do at the field.

ANNABELLE. It's not that, Dickie. Something's happened. Jane, what shall I do?

JANE. (*shaking her head*) It's too hard for me.

ANNABELLE. (*to* JANE) I want to go on this trip more than anything. I was in Poland when the war started; I know the Poles, I could really *do* something on the story. . . .

DICK. What's the matter, Annabelle? I don't get this.

ANNABELLE. I know. And I can't explain. When would we be back, Dickie?

DICK. Tomorrow at the earliest, the day after at the latest. Naturally that's depending on weather.

ANNABELLE. The only forty-eight hours that matter.

DICK. (*puzzled*) What is it, honey? A story? Something you have to work on?

ANNABELLE. Yes. (*pause*) I can't do it, Dickie.

DICK. But you were wild for this trip, Annabelle.

ANNABELLE. I know.

DICK. I was all steamed up about it. It's a screwy idea, but I thought how pretty the sky is at night and I got a kick thinking how you'd like it and all. . . .

ANNABELLE. I'm so ashamed of myself. I've given you so much trouble and now I disappoint you. And I can't even explain. I don't blame you if you never want to speak to me again.

DICK. Don't talk like that. It's been no trouble at all. You're one of the sweetest girls I ever met, and you don't have to explain anything. Whatever you do is O.K. You know that.

(CORPORAL CRAMP *enters.*)

CRAMP. Someone's just rung through, Miss Mason, to say a jeep will be by for you in five minutes. They said please be waiting outside.

JANE. Merciful Heavens! (*jumping out of bed, taking off coat, and putting on skirt*) Sorry, Dickie, but I've got to hurry.

DICK. I better be shoving, myself. If anything happens and you change your mind, Annabelle, I'll be at the REME for another ten minutes.

ANNABELLE. It's such hell the way it's worked out, Dickie. You'll never know how sad I am.

(DICK *exits.*)

ANNABELLE. (*to* JANE) If it had only been tomorrow!

JANE. (*reassuringly*) You can't help it, Annabelle. (*She puts on one sock and begins looking for the other.*)

ANNABELLE. Poor Dickie, after he made all the arrangements and came all the way over here—and I even forgot to wish him luck.

JANE. Dickie thinks everything you do is perfect. Where the devil is my other sock?

ANNABELLE. Look under the duffle bag, or take a pair of mine, on the top of that box. (*reaching for notepaper*) If I write him a note, will you give it to Cramp and ask him to rush it over to the REME? There, Jane, at the bottom of the bed.

JANE. (*pouncing on sock and pulling it on*) Sure. Now where's my toothbrush? (*She picks it up and flies out of the room.*)

(ANNABELLE *sits there scribbling hurriedly. There is furious knocking and* JANE's *voice is heard saying: "For God's sake, hurry. Thank you so much."*)

(*Enter* DAPHNE *in her mink coat.*)

DAPHNE. (*breathlessly*) I'm so sorry to disturb you. I do hope you don't think it's an awful imposition but I've chipped the varnish off one of my nails and it looks so dreadful, I'm in despair, it was so silly of me not to bring any with me, I can't think how I forgot it. . . .

ANNABELLE. (*over-cordial*) Do come in. I think there's some in Jane's dressing-case. Help yourself. There, on the left. (*pause*) Your show must have been a great success last night.

DAPHNE. They were wild about it, poor sweets. I've never sung so many encores in my life, at the end I was an absolute wreck although I must confess it was nothing to the way I felt this morning after that bed I slept on, and no bath, why these Italians don't get the most awful diseases I can't imagine, the dirt in our billet, I'm afraid my skin will never be the same again and just look at my hair. But I suppose it's awfully silly of me to talk to you like this, you probably never think about it. I do think you're wonderful, if I had to stay even one more day . . .

ANNABELLE. (*sweetly*) It's very sad you're leaving.

DAPHNE. How nice of you, but I can't say I'm sorry myself, I only wish we were going now instead of after lunch although with any luck we still might be able to get to Ravello tonight, though Ravello's more romantic in the summer, I must say.

ANNABELLE. I didn't realize you were travelling with someone.

DAPHNE. Oh, I meant Joe. I said to Joe last night I'm under no further obligation to ENSA I really am not. Imagine asking me to take a night off from my own show in Naples to sing in a regiment in reserve, *then* not telling me it was right up there at the front knowing how nervous I am. I said to Joe after this they'll just have to find someone else to take my place for the rest of the week. And I said the Colonel's lending me a car to go down to Naples this afternoon and we can get married tomorrow morning, and I don't care what ENSA says.

ANNABELLE. You're getting married in the morning?

DAPHNE. Perhaps even tonight if there's time, it's all so mad isn't it, you're swept off your feet, everything happens in an absolute whirlwind.

(ANNABELLE *had sprung out of bed and is now looking for her shoes. She proceeds frantically to get ready.*)

DAPHNE. What *has* happened?

ANNABELLE. I've just remembered a date I had at the REME.

(JANE *returns breathless.*)

JANE. I only had time to brush my teeth. Cramp brought enough hot water for a bath. (*Seeing* DAPHNE) Good morning.

ANNABELLE. I haven't time for anything. I've got to meet Dickie. Miss Rutherford's been telling me that she and Joe are leaving for Naples after lunch. They're getting married at once.

DAPHNE. If neither of you want the water it would be absolutely divine to have a bath. I feel so grubby.

JANE. By all means. There's a public towel and soap in there.

DAPHNE. Thank you so much. (*She puts her mink coat and bag on top of trunk.*) *What* a wearing life it is.

(*She exits.*)

JANE. Gloves, gloves, where are they? (*She pushes mink coat off onto box where it is not conspicuous. Then she goes over to* ANNABELLE *and puts her arm around her.*) Darling, Joe's a fool. Have a lovely trip with Dickie.

ANNABELLE. If only he hasn't gone. Here; I've got them.

JANE. You'll make it. Goodbye sweetie. Hope your oxygen mask fits.

ANNABELLE. Don't get your legs blown off, pal. See you in Naples.

JANE. Wait for me if you get there first. Where *is* my lipstick?

(*Exit* JANE.)

(ANNABELLE, *gathering up remnants, exits a second later.*)

(*Enter* CRAMP *with broom. He starts folding blankets on cots, whistling "Lili Marlene."*[17] JOE *comes and stands in the door.*)

ROGERS. Have you seen Miss Rutherford?

CRAMP. No, sir. The other young ladies just left.

ROGERS. Someone said she was up here. I guess she went back to her billet. (ROGERS *enters room and sits wearily on* ANNABELLE's *cot.*) I'm worn out, Cramp.

CRAMP. It's the climate they've got in this country, sir. It's the rain. I never saw such a horrible country.

ROGERS. A man is his own undoing, Cramp, irrespective of climate.

CRAMP. Yes, sir.

ROGERS. Do you have much trouble with women, Cramp?

CRAMP. No, sir.

ROGERS. That's what I like about you.

(ROGERS, *who has been idly looking at some printed matter sees letter on* ANNABELLE's *bed.*)

Who's Major Hawkins?

CRAMP. I don't know him.

ROGERS. I know his name. Let's see? Oh, yes, sure, pilot. I remember. He got the silver star for something, last month. Oh, well.

(ROGERS *opens letter and reads it disinterestedly and leaves it on bed while* CRAMP *goes on sweeping in the corners of the room.*)

What do you think of the war, Cramp?

CRAMP. I think it's a bloody big muck-up, to tell you the truth, sir.

ROGERS. It certainly causes people a lot of trouble.

(*There is a brief silence.*)

I am beginning to regard myself as a psychopathic case, Cramp. I may be war weary, for all I know.

CRAMP. You look all right, sir.

ROGERS. It's my mind. What I say to myself is: How did you ever get in this fix, Rogers my boy, you're not usually such a dumb cluck.

CRAMP. Yes, sir?

ROGERS. And all I do is get in deeper and deeper until you might say the noose is around my neck.

CRAMP. You're not in trouble with the Military, sir?

ROGERS. The Military would be a nice rest. Cramp, listen, would I know if I were going mad? I find myself about to marry a girl that I never intended to marry for one minute. And by God, I bet I get married too.

CRAMP. You wouldn't like it, sir. I mean a man ought to be cheerful at the beginning.

ROGERS. That's easy to say.

CRAMP. Couldn't you explain to the young lady, sir?

ROGERS. That's what I think. But every time I start she talks me down. My Christ, how she talks. (*There is another silence.*) Well, I can make one last desperate try.

CRAMP. Good luck, sir.

ROGERS. I'm worn out, Cramp. When I think I could have stayed in New Guinea where I was having a wonderful time . . .

(*Exit* ROGERS.)

(CRAMP *goes on sweeping for an instant.* TEX *pokes his head in the door.* CRAMP *goes on cleaning and tidying the room.*)

TEX. No-one home?

CRAMP. No, sir.

TEX. Did they say where they were going?

CRAMP. No, sir.

(TEX *enters and looks around the room.*)

TEX. I think the feminine touch has brightened up our little nest, don't you, Cramp?

CRAMP. Yes, I do. It reminds a man what real life's like.

TEX. Even meat and beans taste somewhat better with girls around. You're sure they didn't say where they were going?

CRAMP. No sir. They left together in a great hurry.

TEX. Ah God, I hope they're not working. I have all I can do keeping my eye on the Union Press and now I have to watch the *New York Bulletin* and the *San Francisco World.* People work too much, Cramp.

CRAMP. Yes, sir. Less in the army, I'd say.

TEX. If they come back, tell them I'll be in the Major's office. Waiting for Spring. Has our next whisky ration arrived?

(CRAMP *shakes his head.* TEX *sighs and leaves, and almost immediately* CRAMP *follows him.* DAPHNE *enters. She shivers, picks up a coat of* ANNABELLE's *marked on the sleeve "U.S. War Correspondent," takes* JANE's *dressing-case and sits on the bed and starts to do her hair. At this point* CAPTAIN DRAKE *enters, very hearty.*)

DRAKE. Good morning. Drake's my name. I'm the Conducting Officer.

DAPHNE. Good morning. My name's . . .

DRAKE. You don't need to tell me your name. I know all about you. Blonde hair, blue eyes, and just as pretty as I've heard you were.

DAPHNE. (*bridling*) Have you really heard about me?

DRAKE. Everyone at the front's heard about you. An attractive girl like you can't expect to come up here without creating a sensation, you must know that. All the boys are mad to meet you. In fact the Pictorial Section sent me over this morning to find out whether you'd let them take some pictures.

DAPHNE. How sweet of them, but my hair looks perfectly awful and this uniform's such a mess.

DRAKE. You look all right to me. I wouldn't worry about that. My car's out in front, and any time you're ready . . .

DAPHNE. I didn't realize we had to go somewhere. It's not far, is it? You see I must be back here at twelve. I have a very important engagement.

DRAKE. Not far at all. I'll get you back. You leave everything to me. I'm sorry to say I've only got a jeep, so you'll have to bundle up.

DAPHNE. A jeep! Oh dear. Well, I'd better wear this coat, then. (*Slipping her arms into* ANNABELLE's *coat and picking up her scarf and bag.*) I don't suppose it'll matter. I would hate to ruin my mink.

CURTAIN

Scene Two. Press Camp: early afternoon the same day.

(*When the curtain rises* TEX, ROGERS *and* PHILIP *are on stage.* TEX *is sitting in a comfortable chair by the fire with his feet up;* ROGERS *is walking irritably back and forth across the stage;* PHILIP *is at his desk.*)

TEX. I'd have gone with her, or Hank. All you had to do was mention it.

PHILIP. I told you Drake isn't taking her anywhere near the front. He was going somewhere north of here where she'd imagine it was the front.

TEX. Philip, you're a good guy but sometimes you get so olde worlde it makes me sick. It's half-witted to talk as if Jane wouldn't know the difference between the front and someplace near the front. If she went out with Drake, she went to the front. Don't be so goddamn stupid about it.

PHILIP. If you can't control your . . .

TEX. Okay, okay. But I like Jane, see? And I know Drake, and I know those roads. If you have to be loyal to your conducting officer that's fine with me, but it's no reason to get my friends bumped off.

(*Enter* CRAMP *via outside door.*)

CRAMP. The driver says shall he wait any longer. It's the jeep to take Miss Jones to Naples.

PHILIP. Certainly he's to wait.

(*Exit* CRAMP *via outside door.*)

ROGERS. (*paying no attention to* TEX) I don't understand where Daphne could be. It doesn't make sense, that's all. Somebody in this Press Camp might know where somebody is some of the time.

PHILIP. I am *not* responsible for Miss Rutherford.

ROGERS. All right. You're not responsible for her. Then will you kindly tell me where Annabelle is? Or aren't you responsible for her either?

(CRAMP *returns with a pair of khaki trousers over his arm. From outside [a gramophone recording] a fierce argument starts between a man and a woman in Italian. The voices fill the room.*)

PHILIP. Cramp, for God's sake get rid of those people.

CRAMP. (*leaning out of the window*) Basta. (*Nothing happens.*) Didn't you hear me say Basta? Go on now. Move away from there. (*The voices continue.*)

ROGERS. We could even have an Italian interpreter attached to this outfit if anyone had the foresight of a flea.

CRAMP. Basta. Shut up. (*inspired, pointing to mouth*) Eat. Kitchen. (*making frantic gestures*) Marcha la cucina. Cucina. Come on, don't dawdle. (*The voices dwindle—with sounds of "Grazie Signor" floating up.*)

(*Exit* CRAMP *via outside door.*)

(*The telephone rings.*)

PHILIP. Hello. Yes. (*listens*) Please tell General Pinkerton that neither Miss Mason nor Miss Jones are here at the moment. Oh, I didn't realize it was you speaking, sir. Major Brooke-Jervaux, sir. Yes, sir, I don't know exactly where they are. There are a good many correspondents staying here. (*pause*) I'm not trying to make excuses, sir. She did go with a conducting officer. I don't know where Miss Jones is. No, she didn't go with a conducting officer. I'm very sorry, sir. I realize it does no good. I'm very sorry. Very well, sir, I won't say I'm sorry. (*pause while* PHILIP *listens*) (*then furious*) He's hung up. You'd think I'd lost them on purpose.

(*Trucks pass in the street. They raise their voices to speak.*)

ROGERS. It doesn't seem to occur to you that Daphne's disappeared too.

PHILIP. What in hell can I do about Daphne? Why didn't you look after her yourself?

TEX. Anyway she won't have gone to the front, that's one sure thing. (*pause*) I wonder if Jane and Annabelle could be on to anything.

ROGERS. (*anxiously*) What is there? The attack starts tomorrow.

TEX. I don't know.

(HANK *bursts into the room.*)

HANK. The boys have something good for a change. They're typing away like hell in there. (*He goes to* DRAKE's *machine, types as he talks.*) Seems the Germans allowed a limited truce for one ambulance to pick up wounded on Mount Sorello.

TEX. Go on! More!

HANK. That's all I know. Very poor reporters those young men.

TEX. What hospital did they go to?

HANK. That evac hospital down Route Six. The nearest one, so the boys say.

(TEX *dashes towards* PHILIP's *desk.*)

PHILIP. I'm sitting here, Tex.

TEX. Just one minute, old boy.

PHILIP. No, dammit, use your own typewriter.

TEX. (*to* HANK) Has anybody got this through yet?

HANK. No.

(*exit to Press Room door*)

HANK. Hello, Operator, I want Freedom rear. Okay, try it via Primrose. I don't care how you get in. Look son, this is a news bulletin. Don't let's have a ways and means committee, shall we? Just try ringing them—By the way, Philip, Jane went.

PHILIP. *What!*

HANK. So the boys say. They got the dope from the field dressing station. Seems they saw her drive by in the ambulance.

PHILIP. Good God!

HANK. Nothing to worry about. She'll be down at the Evac Hospital with the wounded. (HANK *is typing as he talks.*)

PHILIP. How can she have . . .

ROGERS. What gets me is how these women find things out! I think every goddamn officer in Italy spends his time blabbing to women. They run this lousy war on sex-appeal.

(*Two shells land distantly. People only speak louder.*)

PHILIP. (*at other phone*) Is the Evac Hospital of Route Six on this exchange? Good. Put me through please. I want to speak to the C.O. Give me his adjutant, then. Major Brooke-Jervaux here, Press Camp. Is Miss Mason at the hospital? No, not a nurse. She's a war correspondent. Because she went up to Mount Sorello with your ambulance. Surely you know if your own ambulance is back or not? Would you mind looking? (*pause; to the room: "They never heard of her."*)

HANK. Freedom rear? Give me 91634. Hello, who's that? Monahan? O'Reilly here. How you doing, boy? Listen, I want to send a bulletin through, but quick. Take it down for me, will you? Ready? "Unpress ex O'Reilly Italfront bulletin German agree hours truce cumus forces surrounded engarrison Mount Sorello prooutbringing."[18] Okay. Are you writing with your feet?

PHILIP. (*to telephone*) You can't act as if it were a military secret whether a woman is at your hospital or is *not* at your hospital. (*furious*) Well, then where in hell *is* your Colonel? All right, ask him to call me, if he's ever found. (PHILIP *hangs up telephone.*)

PHILIP. (*grimly*) If anything's happened to that girl . . .

ROGERS. It's got so a man hasn't a prayer to get a story.

HANK. (*noticing* PHILIP's *expression*) Don't get excited. She'll show up. Monahan! (*louder*) Monahan! They've cut me off! Operator! I was talking to freedom rear.

(*Phone rings on* P.R. *desk.*)

PHILIP. Hello. Colonel Wutzenbaum? Yes, I've heard the report. I don't know whether it's true yet. (*pause, and then growing angry*) What does your office mean allowing women up here in the first place? Nobody asked acceptance from me. I will not take that, sir. Miss Jones was here this morning. No, I don't know where Miss Jones is. No doubt Miss Jones has parachuted behind the German lines and is now operating with the Italian guerillas. I am not making a joke. Furthermore, we have a third woman missing, in case you're interested. I am not taking it lightly, I am suggesting that women should not have been allowed here in the first place. It may be entirely forgotten in Naples but a war is being waged in this neighbourhood. I am not being insolent, sir. Very well, I'll inform you at once.

HANK. (*anguished*) Freedom rear. Give me 91634.

ROGERS. You don't really think Annabelle's gone off on something?

HANK. I think she's lecturing to the Poggibonsi Women's Club.

ROGERS. (*inspiration dawning*) Hawkins!

HANK. (*with relief*) Monahan! I never thought I'd hear your lovely voice again.

ROGERS. (*snapping fingers*) Hawkins! Special missions! I bet that's it!

(ROGERS *dashes out of the room via hall door.*)

HANK. "Prooutbringing." Got that? "U.S. German wounded fifty hyphen fifty basis stop lone ambulance exour lines allowable itall taken U.S. 106 Evachospital." Got it? Check with the Censor while I hold on, will you. And *move* on. (*to* PHILIP) What a story Jane'll have!

PHILIP. You're all mad! You don't seem to realize the danger. What if anything's happened to her? The Germans may have stopped her at a road block. She could be a prisoner for all we know.

HANK. You *are* worried, pal.

PHILIP. No one wants anything to happen to a woman.

HANK. Okay Monahan? Buy you a drink some day. Hurry it, will you? So long.

(ROGERS *enters with* ANNABELLE's *letter in his hand.*)

HANK. Now I've got to catch up with Tex. Little Jane's a smart girl, isn't she?

ROGERS. They're both too damn smart. (*pointing to letter*) I'll be hearing about this from my editor.

(*Enter* JANE *from outside door, with wet hair and coat, looking tired, muddy with some bloodstains on her coat.*)

JANE. (*in a small voice*) Hello.

ROGERS. Jane! (*He stuffs letter in his pocket.*)

HANK. Oh daughter!

PHILIP. Thank God you're all right.

HANK. Come here, you lovely little thing. Sit down near the stove. How do you feel? (*He puts* JANE *into one of the two large chairs.*) Now tell us all about it.

JANE. There isn't anything to tell.

HANK. Honey, don't be stingy. You know I can't use your kind of stuff. How many men are up there? How's the ammunition holding out? How do they handle the wounded? Come on, you can spare me a few little things.

PHILIP. (*with the crossness that comes from immense relief*) I'm very relieved to see you've come back safely, Miss Mason. Will you please explain how you went to Mount Sorello without permission?

JANE. I didn't go to Mount Sorello. I sat in a ditch with Captain Drake.

PHILIP. What was Drake doing in a ditch?

JANE. (*wearily*) Let's start at the beginning. I was bowling along in the ambulance about a mile beyond our lines. Steve was driving fast because he had to collect the wounded before everyone started shooting again. We saw someone waving and when we slowed down we could hear screaming.

PHILIP. Screaming?

JANE. Yes, good old-fashioned screaming. That was Daphne.

ROGERS. Daphne? Is she hurt?

JANE. Not much. I slapped her, and Steve slapped her, and Drake would have slapped her if he'd had the strength.

ROGERS. I don't get it. Why was Drake there, and why was he there with Daphne?

JANE. He was there because he thought he was on a quiet unused lateral road four kilometres behind the front. The Germans let him come for a while; and then they opened up with an 88, and one of them got him. He couldn't hold the jeep and it skidded over in a ditch and the reason he had Daphne there was because he thought she was me, that is, until she started screaming. . . .

(*An aeroplane comes over. Loud noise. They raise their voices.*)

ROGERS. Where is she now?

JANE. On Mount Sorello.

PHILIP *and* ROGERS. (*horrified*) *What?*

JANE. What else could we do with her? She was having hysterics and we couldn't leave her alone with Drake. He was hurt and needed looking after. So we pushed her in the rear of the ambulance and Steve took off and I lost my story, and that's that.

PHILIP. Why didn't the ambulance bring her back?

JANE. Don't be silly. They had that ambulance packed to the roof. Drake and I got back in a Red Cross jeep Steve sent out for us when he'd finished.

PHILIP. Why do those insane things? (*bitterly*) You're famous enough already.

JANE. (*very angry*) I could write the Society Column in New York if I wanted to. (*to* HANK) Steve didn't have much time to talk but he said they're solid as rock up there and good, and making jokes.

HANK. It would have been a great story if you'd got there. I don't like to leave Tex alone at the Evac Hospital. See you later.

(*Exit* HANK.)

(*Enter* CRAMP.)

CRAMP. There's a Colonel from the hospital on the Press Room telephone, sir.

PHILIP. It's nice they've found their Colonel again. Tell him I'm busy. No, I'll have to speak to him. (*bitterly*) Colonels . . .

(*Exit* PHILIP *via Press Room door.*)

CRAMP. Can I do anything for you, Miss?

JANE. No thank you, Corporal.

(*Exit* CRAMP *via outside door.*)

ROGERS. (*gloomily*) On Mount Sorello. Oh Lord, what a mess I'm in.

JANE. What a mess *you're* in! You'd *have* to be a man to see it like that.

ROGERS. You don't understand. If it hadn't been for me Daphne wouldn't be in Italy now. I'm responsible.

JANE. It's certainly a back-breaking responsibility. (*softening*) She'll be all right, Joe. They'll put her in a good deep cellar.

ROGERS. That's not the point. After this, how can I ever get out of it?

JANE. Out of what?

ROGERS. (*crossly*) Can't you understand? I've been looking for Daphne all morning to tell her it's all off. But when she comes back from this rat-race, shellshocked, or wounded, or God knows what, how can I ever break it? I'm stuck.

JANE. I'm willing to bet you'll find a way.

ROGERS. (*ignoring her*) A man does a lot of silly things I suppose a woman would never do. Minute I saw Annabelle I knew it was a mistake.

JANE. It's a pity one never knows until too late, isn't it?

ROGERS. But maybe it isn't too late. If I could only find Annabelle and talk to her, I know she'd help me. We could fix something up together.

JANE. You know Annabelle has dozens of men in love with her, though of course it's none of my business.

ROGERS. Jane, you must know where she is.

JANE. I'm sorry, I really haven't the faintest idea.

ROGERS. Listen Jane, if Annabelle was here and a man came along who was crazy in love with you and worried sick and asked her where you were she'd tell him.

JANE. She certainly wouldn't. We're very good friends.

ROGERS. Then I'll have to get busy on the telephone.

JANE. (*alarmed*) Who're you going to call?

ROGERS. I don't know. I'll start ringing around. Divisions. Brigades. Perhaps some of the airfields.

JANE. (*cajoling*) Don't be silly, Joe. Annabelle will be back.

ROGERS. (*quickly*) I thought you said you didn't know where she was.

JANE. I don't. When I left this morning she was still in bed. But she always does show up.

ROGERS. Ever hear of a fellow called Hawkins?

JANE. I know dozens of Hawkinses.

ROGERS. This one's a pretty good pilot. I didn't remember who he was at first either. His squadron does special jobs. The other day when I was over at Foggia they were talking about a mission to Poland. (*watches* JANE's *face*)

JANE. Really I've got enough problems without worrying over unknown characters planning unknown trips to unknown destinations.

ROGERS. Strange you don't know this fellow. He seems to be a buddy of Annabelle's.

(JOE *takes* ANNABELLE's *letter out of his pocket.*)

JANE. (*recognizing it*) Where'd you get that? What d'you mean stealing people's letters?

(*Enter* PHILIP, *behind them, from Press Room.*)

ROGERS. All right, then, just tell me. Annabelle's gone to Poland, hasn't she?

JANE. Give me that.

PHILIP. Poland! It's not possible.

ROGERS. It sure is, pal. Didn't you know this war was run on sex-appeal? No other correspondent has ever gone to Poland but then most correspondents don't look like Miss Jones.

JANE. (*to* ROGERS) You're absolutely revolting.

PHILIP. Your ideas about war, Miss Mason, are too peculiar to discuss. You find it perfectly normal to secrete yourself in an ambulance and rush off to a surrounded mountain. You also think it normal for Miss Jones to ignore all regulations which apply to the Press and depart for Poland. There is an end to what can go on, even with women. (*He starts for the phone*) Do you know what field she's on, Rogers?

ROGERS. No.

(PHILIP *picks up the phone.*)

JANE. What are you going to do?

PHILIP. I'm going to call AFHQ[19] Public Relations at Caserta and inform them of this and they can take what action they like.

JANE. They'd stop her trip.

PHILIP. I should hope so.

JANE. They'd do something awful to Dickie.

PHILIP. I don't know who Dickie is, but I imagine he'll be court-martialled.

JANE. They might take Annabelle's credentials away.

PHILIP. They certainly might. There has to be some discipline somewhere.

JANE. And you intend to telephone them?

PHILIP. As you see.

JANE. (*rising*) All right. Go ahead. Ruin everybody. I hope you're very proud of yourself, and I hope you're delighted too, Mr. Rogers. I hope you burst with satisfaction, both of you. You don't care about anything except your own measly little authority, and all Joe can think about is what a jam he's in with Daphne, and whether Annabelle will get a better story than he ever got, just because she's a woman. That's all you care about the war. It doesn't occur to you that Annabelle is going on this trip because she can do a good job. She knows about the Poles. They haven't any Press of their own to tell their story in. She'll do something wonderful for them. But you couldn't be expected to care about that. You only care about credentials and permission and whether everyone's got travel orders. You seem to think she's gone on this trip just to cause you trouble. And if she got killed or captured or deformed for life you'd only be furious because she hadn't done it through the proper channels.

(JANE *slams out of the room. There is a silence. Both men light cigarettes.*)

PHILIP. (*holding the phone*) What if she *does* get killed?

ROGERS. She won't. She's not that kind of a girl.

PHILIP. Oh God, I wish I were back in the Tanks.

ROGERS. I'm going to get drunk. If I can find anything to do it with. And then I'm going to write a good long think-piece.

(ROGERS *starts towards kitchen.*)

PHILIP. Tell Cramp I want him, will you?

(ROGERS *exits via outside door.*)

(*Telephone on desk rings.*)

PHILIP. Oh, Operator? No, it's a mistake. (*He slowly puts the telephone back in box.*)

(CRAMP *enters.*)

CRAMP. You sent for me, sir?

PHILIP. Have you any hot water?

CRAMP. Yes sir.

PHILIP. Take some up to Miss Mason.

(CRAMP *starts to exit.*)

And Cramp, you might tell her not to worry about Miss Jones.

(CRAMP *exits via outside door.*)

(*There is the sound of shells landing, fairly loud.* PHILIP *gets up and goes over to the stove. Enter* TEX *and* HANK *from outside door.* CRAMP *passes through the room with kettle of hot water.*)

TEX. Hello, Philip. Wonderful guys those wounded. Gave us all the dope on Mount Sorello. Plenty of colour, too. Names and addresses. Nice little story. Everybody's happy.

HANK. Drake sent you his love, Philip. He looks a little green but the doctor says he'll be all right.

TEX. Drake said: "Tell Philip I'm perfectly fit old boy, don't you know. I'll be quite ready to escort the chaps around in another week."

HANK. He told us about Jane. What a girl!

PHILIP. What about Miss Mason?

HANK. Nothing except she handled the whole thing like a little angel. She saw Drake was in a bad way and she just popped out of the ambulance and took over. He said it was a wonder how that girl knew all the first-aid business. She got the stuff out of the ambulance it seems. Gave him morphine, cut off his clothes, sulfaed the wounds. He said he couldn't have anything better in a cracking fine hospital. His own words, almost.

TEX. They took a good pasting, too. A couple of shells landed so near Drake says it gave him the shakes.

(*Enter* LEONARD.)

TEX. Hello, old boy. What's new?

LEONARD. I've been to the briefing at Corps. The Brigadier was rather displeased that none of you bothered to come. I stayed for lunch and got some quite useful information.

HANK. I'm too shy to eat with Brigadiers.

LEONARD. Rogers is in the kitchen drinking cognac straight from the bottle. He says Miss Rutherford hasn't gone to Naples after all. Is she around here by any chance?

TEX. You mean to say you don't know about Daphne? You're slipping, Leonard! Why, right this minute that sweet little girl is up on Mount Sorello, singing to our boys.

LEONARD. She couldn't be.

HANK. Sure she is. She worked her way up in an ambulance. Ask anyone. Ring the hospital.

LEONARD. (*riveted with admiration*) And she said she was so frightened! I never really believed her. I can tell the type of person who's modest about being brave.

(*He hurries out to the Press Room.*)

(*The others look at him, puzzled.*)

HANK. The thing about Leonard is he'll believe anything.

TEX. Well, it's always pleasant to talk to you men, but I've got a little work to do. Mind if I use your typewriter, Philip?

PHILIP. Yes, I do.

TEX. Thanks all the same.

HANK. I guess the dope on Mount Sorello goes first, don't you, Tex?

TEX. The Censor'll kill most of it anyway. . . .

(*They go out of the Press Room door.*)

(PHILIP *goes over, gets a bottle of whisky from behind the books on the shelf and pours himself a drink. The telephone rings. He answers it angrily.*)

PHILIP. Major Brooke-Jervaux speaking. Public Relations Caserta? (*wearily*) I was expecting that. Never mind. Yes, I'm ready. (*pause*) Good afternoon, General Bumper. Yes, sir. Miss Mason is here, sir. (*pause*) But sir, she didn't actually get to the garrison. . . . (*pause*) But sir, I'd like to point out . . . (*Pause*) But sir, you don't understand, there was an accident and she stayed behind to help a wounded officer. She saved his life, actually. (*pause, exercised*) But surely, sir, that's too drastic under the circumstances.

(JANE *enters the room and stands near hall door unnoticed.*)

She wasn't trying to get round the censorship or anything like that. If you take away her credentials she can't work in any theatre of war. (*with icy anger*) If you do take such a step, sir, I shall feel obliged to make an official protest to Corps and ask that a detailed favourable report be sent to the theatre commander. In my opinion it would be a great injustice. Yes sir, I'll see that you get all the facts.

JANE. Oh, *please* don't get into trouble because of me. I'm sorry I couldn't help overhearing what you said. I came down to thank you for Annabelle and now I'm the one. It's terribly kind, but I can't let you . . .

PHILIP. (*embarrassed*) It's nothing. Bumper wouldn't come up and take a look at the war himself on a bet. He's got no right to punish people who are only doing their job.

JANE. But you *can't* get into trouble because of me. I'd hate losing my credentials, but it doesn't really matter. I was planning to go to America anyway.

PHILIP. Nonsense. It's ridiculous to let Bumper get away with a thing like this. It's a question of principle.

JANE. Well, it's—it's wonderful of you. I don't know how to thank you. (*remorsefully*) And after what I said to you.

PHILIP. I understand why you were angry. (*pause*) I think you were right.

JANE. I wasn't right. (*pause; embarrassed silence*) I'd better finish cleaning up. (*She starts to leave.*)

PHILIP. (*impulsively*) Don't go.

JANE. But I'm so dirty.

PHILIP. (*embarrassed at having been so dashing*) If I'm going to write that report I'll need a few more details. I say, you've still got on those wet shoes. Come over and sit by the stove.

(JANE *follows* PHILIP *to the stove. She sits down and kicks off her shoes.*)

PHILIP. I'll get you a drink. Don't burn your feet.

JANE. (*stretching out her feet towards the stove*) Oh my! This *is* an improvement.

PHILIP. (*pouring drink at his desk*) I hear you put up a good show this morning.

JANE. I didn't do anything. I just sat.

PHILIP. That's not what Drake says.

JANE. (*laughing*) Drake is a big brave clown.

PHILIP. Here you are.

(*He gives* JANE *her glass and sits down beside her.*)

JANE. What do you want to know?

(PHILIP *looks puzzled.*)

The report.

PHILIP. Oh yes, the report. How long have you been a war correspondent?

JANE. Seven years. I started in the Spanish War.

PHILIP. (*astounded*) But you were a child! How could your family let you?

JANE. Father? I didn't ask him of course. He wouldn't remember if I had. He's too busy with his research on encephalitis lethargica. I doubt if he noticed I wasn't there for a year or two.

PHILIP. But surely he worries about your travelling around alone. You must run into all sorts of complications.

JANE. No more than anyone else. Just the usual army tiresomeness.

PHILIP. I mean with men.

JANE. At least there's only one General Bumper.

PHILIP. (*determined*) No, I mean with men being personal.

JANE. That isn't much of a problem. Annabelle and I weren't attacked last night.

PHILIP. Naturally you're safe here. Foreigners are different.

(*Two shells land loud and fairly close.*)

JANE. (*seriously*) In peacetime in Venice I remember the Italians pinched one quite a lot. That sort of thing seems to have gone out with the war.

(CRAMP *enters from outside with kerosene tin.*)

CRAMP. I thought I'd fill the stove, sir.

PHILIP. Later.

CRAMP. Yes sir. Some shells are landing long in the village sir. They're trying for the convoys.

PHILIP. Thank you, Cramp.

(CRAMP *exits via outside door.*)

JANE. (*flirtatiously*) Is there anything else you'd like to know?

PHILIP. (*first puzzled, then embarrassed*) Oh yes. I intend to say this is the first time you've had any trouble with the authorities.

JANE. But I always have trouble with the authorities.

PHILIP. Do you? I'd better not mention it, then. You're terribly independent, aren't you?

JANE. (*with wide, innocent eyes*) Only when absolutely necessary.

(PHILIP *pauses, baffled.*)

PHILIP. Did you mean that about going to America?

JANE. Yes, I think it will be such fun. On a bucket-seat in an unheated transport.

PHILIP. You really oughtn't to go yet. The front will start moving when the mud dries. Someone's got to report what's going on, and there are so few first class correspondents to do it.

JANE. That's a very nice speech. But you know I want to be quiet and live in one place for a while.

PHILIP. If it were only peacetime I'd ask you to come to Frampton Towers. That's where I live in Yorkshire. You could be very quiet there. Perhaps the quiet would bore you.

JANE. Oh no, I adore the country. I've always loved the Riviera.

(*Four shells land, loud and fairly near.*)

PHILIP. Yorkshire's rather a different sort of country. Probably you're homesick for America.

JANE. (*amazed*) Oh no, I'm never homesick. I don't mind what country I live in as long as it's comfortable.

PHILIP. I suppose the English are different. We're terribly fixed about homes. I'm always miserable if I stay away from Frampton for long.

JANE. You've been away a long time now?

PHILIP. Three years. I'd love to show you the rose garden.

JANE. What rose garden?

PHILIP. At Frampton. It sounds silly, but I've been remembering it since yesterday as if I were looking at it.

JANE. (*politely*) I'd love to see it.

PHILIP. I—you'd—it would be very becoming to you . . .

(*He breaks off in a sudden and embarrassed silence. More shells land, always nearer.*)

JANE. (*easily*) My feet are warm for the first time since I've been here.

(*There is a pause during which Jane sips her drink, looking pleased, and* PHILIP *looks restless and unhappy.*)

PHILIP. As a rule, I never find much to talk about with women. You start out full of optimism, and then you're bored stiff. I go to London, planning to be gay, and end up in my club. I've never met one I could talk to before.

JANE. You must be a difficult man to please.

PHILIP. (*flattered*) That's why it's extraordinary to meet someone like you.

JANE. You didn't think so yesterday.

PHILIP. I didn't know what you were like yesterday. I had a lot of silly ideas about women war correspondents. (*pause*) I suppose you have dozens of men bothering you to death.

JANE. I haven't noticed it. What about you? Cramp tells me the women are queued up in Yorkshire, waiting for you.

PHILIP. Cramp couldn't have said that!

JANE. I suppose it must be the way you lead them on.

PHILIP. Good God! You don't think I talk to other women like this?

JANE. No?

PHILIP. You know, I can't make you out. You're not like an English girl, but you're not really American. I mean most American women are married and divorced half a dozen times before they're twenty. I don't believe in divorce myself. I think people should wait until they're sure.

JANE. It's not always easy to tell.

PHILIP. I think it is. I think you know at once.

JANE. (*looking him full into the eyes; the works*) Do you?

(PHILIP *stares at her, helplessly and unable to think of the essential next step. There is a near loud explosion and plaster falls in dust and small chunks from the ceiling.*)

PHILIP. (*stricken, as if something terrible had happened*) You've got plaster in your hair. (*He starts to brush it off.*)

(JANE's *face is turned up, and suddenly he takes her head in both hands and kisses her.*)

JANE. You've got plaster in your hair, too.

PHILIP. I've been longing to do that. I'm in love with you, Jane.

JANE. But how can you? You don't know me.

PHILIP. I've been in love with you for forty-five minutes.

(*There is an explosion, and again the house shakes.* PHILIP's *arms tighten around* JANE.)

If we could only stay like this, alone and quiet, with nothing to bother us.

JANE. It *is* lovely, isn't it?

(PHILIP *puts his hand on her chin and turns her face up to his.*)

JANE. Even when you were so cross to me . . .

PHILIP. (*gently*) Stop talking. . . .

(*He kisses her again, this time long and passionately. There are three loud explosions, the house shakes violently; windows rattle, tables shake and there is the sound of pots and pans falling in the kitchen, but* JANE *and* PHILIP *never move.*)

CURTAIN

Act Three
Forward Press Camp: The next morning.

Throughout this Act there is the intermittent noise of tanks, trucks, etc., rolling up to the front, and distant artillery.

(*When the curtain rises,* ROGERS, TEX, HANK *and* CRAMP *are on stage.*)

CRAMP. There seems to be one for all the gentlemen. Here's yours, sir. (*He hands a cable to* ROGERS.) Shall I leave Miss Mason's here, sir?

(TEX *and* HANK *are reading cables.*)

ROGERS. That's all right.

    (*Exit* CRAMP *with more cables via Press Room door.*)

HANK. They can't be that dumb.

TEX. (*carefully*) What's yours about?

HANK. Daphne. "Get immediate interview famous English actress century's bravest stage personality."

TEX. So my office isn't the only loony bin in New York.

ROGERS. (*reading*) "Unable understand how uncovered Daphne Rutherford send full story fastest."

TEX. It must be wonderful to sit in New York with your finger on the pulse of the world—always seeing the big issues—far-sighted, clear-headed.

HANK. Did you send anything on that dame?

TEX. Now listen, Hank.

HANK. Rogers?

ROGERS. What do you take me for?

HANK. The sports writers wouldn't have. They're too busy writing their military hash. (*pause*) It's Leonard.

TEX. (*laughing*) The correspondent's correspondent! I am going to give Leonard a present some day. Well, back to the mines. Old Tex Crowder has no time to waste with you lugs.

(TEX *sits down at Drake's typewriter.* HANK *and* ROGERS *are lounging about smoking cigarettes and stalling off the moment when they have to work.*)

HANK. (*to* ROGERS) It was a fine piece of work, this time.

ROGERS. I never saw anything prettier than those P-47's working on the gun positions on the left flank.

HANK. Did you see the one that copped it?

ROGERS. I saw him start his dive but I didn't see him crash.

HANK. They were a good tough bunch of kids up there.

ROGERS. Yeh.

TEX. How do you like this? (*reading*) "Your correspondent reached unyielding American garrison Mount Sorello in company first infantry platoon smashing German death grip."

HANK. Now listen, brother.

TEX. There's no use going into a lot of detail about how I got there a half hour or so after the corridor was opened.

(*Enter* JANE *from hall door; she is wearing a khaki sweater with her uniform skirt, and a camouflage parachute silk scarf around her throat. She looks rested and pretty, but distressed.*)

JANE. You're not back, are you? It's not all over, is it?

TEX. The main show's over. They're widening the corridor now.

HANK. The krauts were counter-attacking on the left flank but it didn't look like much.

JANE. Oh God, how can Cramp have let me sleep?

HANK. I'd have called you, honey, if you'd said anything.

JANE. I told Cramp, that's why. How were the boys up there?

HANK. 106 living, 52 wounded, 65 dead. The living were very cheerful.

JANE. Are they all out now?

HANK. Most of them. They've taken them back to some lousy wet tents to rest.

TEX. And when the heroic defenders return to America, five or six years after the campaign in Italy is over, they will tell their friends and relatives of this action. And their friends and relatives will say: "Mount Sorello? Mount Sorello? Never heard of it, son."

ROGERS. It always makes Tex bitter to get up early. There's a service message for you, Jane.

JANE. It makes me sick to have missed it. (*reading her telegram*) Oh, it's not possible. The fools! I'll send them the hottest answer they ever got!

TEX. (*happily*) What does yours say?

JANE. (*reading*) "Where were you while Daphne Rutherford went to Mount Sorello?"

(*The* MEN *laugh.*)

(*furious*) It's not funny, and now I've missed the attack too. I might as well be in Algiers.

HANK. We got queries too, Janie. It's Leonard. He must have filed some half-witted story yesterday.

JANE. Where is she, anyway? Are you going to write about her?

HANK. Hell, no. I'm covering a war, not running a gossip column. One of the boys said she came out with the first load of wounded. We didn't see her.

(TEX, *who has been typing intermittently during the conversation, now picks up the field telephone on Drake's desk.*)

TEX. Hello, Operator, get me Freedom rear. What? You mean to say one lousy night's rain and all the lines in the lousy country are down? What in hell are we paying the engineers for? No, I don't want to speak to Caserta. I want to speak to Naples. It's certainly nice to hear they've still got some contact with the outside world at Caserta. No, I don't want to speak to people just because they happen to have a telephone that works. Oh, nuts.

ROGERS. Dispatch riders. (*He opens the Press Room door and calls*) Philip!

JANE. I can't get over missing *everything*.

ROGERS. *Philip!*

PHILIP'S VOICE. I'm coming. You don't have to shout the house down.

(PHILIP *enters*.)

ROGERS. The telephone.

PHILIP. I know all about it. I've got dispatch riders laid on. The first one will leave here in ten minutes.

JANE. (*with special smile*) Good morning, Major.

PHILIP. (*shy, but beaming*) Good morning.

HANK. Can I use your typewriter, Philip?

PHILIP. No. Will you all be good enough to use the Press Room, for a change. I have some work to do.

(TEX *takes his story from the typewriter and he and* HANK *go out via the Press Room door.*)

ROGERS. If we're lucky the dispatch rider won't lose himself and all our stories and show up in Naples tomorrow night.

PHILIP. (*coldly*) That only happened once.

ROGERS. It isn't as if we had something decent to write every day.

(*Exit* ROGERS *via Press Room door, and* (*enter* CRAMP *from hall door, carrying a typewriter and folding canvas army suitcase.*)

CRAMP. Mr. Lightfoot's luggage, sir. He telephoned to have it downstairs.

(CRAMP *prepares to deposit luggage.*)

PHILIP. Is Mr. Lightfoot leaving? He hasn't bothered to inform me. Put it in the front hall, Cramp.

PHILIP. (*waiting until* CRAMP *has left, then putting his arms around* JANE) Good morning, darling. Did you get a good rest?

JANE. Good morning, Philip. Oh, Philip, it's too shaming. I can't say I overslept. Whoever heard of missing an attack? How can Cramp have forgotten?

PHILIP. Don't blame Cramp, darling. I told him to let you sleep.

JANE. You didn't!

PHILIP. You had a hard day yesterday, and you need the rest.

JANE. Oh, Philip!

PHILIP. I can't have you going to the front any more, Jane.

JANE. But my paper. I'm the only correspondent they've got out here.

PHILIP. (*putting his arm around her and leading her to sofa*) Surely you're not worried about what some ridiculous paper expects you to do.

JANE. My paper isn't ridiculous, Philip.

PHILIP. It seems a little ridiculous to let it interfere with what *we* want.

JANE. But yesterday you said there were so few experienced correspondents and how important it was . . .

PHILIP. (*taking her hand*) You must see it's changed. You're mine now. If anything happened to you I couldn't stand it.

(JANE *looks partly cross and partly mollified.*)

PHILIP. I've thought about it all night and I think I've got the answer. I'm due to be transferred any time now, and with the second front coming on it's certain to be England. It would be wonderful if you'd stay with mother and Emily in Yorkshire until we can get married.

JANE. Emily?

PHILIP. My sister. You'll love her, and she'll adore you.

JANE. (*uncertain*) Do you think so? Oh, Philip, I don't think I could do that.

PHILIP. It's perfectly normal, darling. You're my fiancée. And you'd get plenty of butter and milk and you need to fatten up a bit.

JANE. I don't want to fatten up.

PHILIP. I don't want you to be fat, you little silly, but not *so* thin. It would do you a lot of good, and I wouldn't worry about you, and it would be lovely for Mother and Emily.

JANE. But, Philip . . .

PHILIP. I've got a command car to take you down to Naples. Bumper telephoned again and says you're to stop at Caserta. He's quieted down all right, you won't have any trouble with him. He says he only wants to give you a talking to. You'll have to leave here at noon. I'll meet you this evening, and we'll have dinner at Angelo's, and tomorrow morning I'll put you on a plane for Algiers and you can go right on from there to England.

JANE. But . . .

PHILIP. Darling, look at me. (*He kisses her.*) See? You don't have to think of a thing. All you have to do is pack.

JANE. (*smiling*) It just shows what a P.R. can do when he wants to.

(DAPHNE *enters from street door with a smart borrowed army coat, an American flag and a German helmet in her hand.* LEONARD, *very pleased, is trailing behind.*)

DAPHNE. Hello, everybody!

LEONARD. Here she is, safe and sound.

DAPHNE. Oh, Miss Mason, so you're all right are you? I was wondering whether you'd ever got back again, the last time I saw Miss Mason was in a ditch, imagine! I don't believe I know you, do I?

LEONARD. Major Brooke-Jervaux.

DAPHNE. Oh, you're the P.R., then you know everything. Poor Captain Drake talked about you, he was a mess he really was, bleeding all over, I hated leaving Miss Mason with him but I'm simply no good in situations like that, I faint dead away, I've been like that ever since I was a child and Miss Mason was so calm, exactly like a man if you know what I mean, she never turned a hair, so I thought it was better for her to stay behind and let me go on up to the garrison.

PHILIP. I'm extremely sorry Drake took you to the front. It was all a mistake and I'd like to say how . . .

DAPHNE. Oh don't apologize, please don't apologize. Naturally at first I was a little upset but when I got up there and saw how pleased the boys were I wouldn't have missed the experience for anything, poor sweets, they hadn't even seen a woman for eight days, you can't imagine how thrilled they were, it's really terrible what people go through in this war.

(*Enter* TEX *and* HANK *from Press Room door.*)

TEX. Where's that bloody dispatch rider? (*seeing* DAPHNE) Our heroine!

DAPHNE. You mustn't praise me, I really don't deserve anything, it's all those wonderful American boys.

TEX. Oh I don't know. Think what you meant to them. You probably gave them that final ounce of courage.

HANK. The bravest stage personality of the century, that's what my Editor called you.

DAPHNE. Oh did he really? He shouldn't have. I was only doing my bit, I'm devoted to the Americans you know, you can't think how friendly they all were. . . .

LEONARD. Daphne!

DAPHNE. What's the matter with you?

LEONARD. You seem to have forgotten our agreement.

DAPHNE. Leonard doesn't want me to talk. He says I'm signed up exclusively, it's all so complicated, I don't understand any of it, my head's spinning with all the things that happen.

LEONARD. Daphne, we've really got to be going. Do you want anything besides your coat?

DAPHNE. No, I don't believe so. It's upstairs I think.

LEONARD. I'll get it for you.

(LEONARD *exits, with an uneasy look, through the hall door.*)

DAPHNE. I must say it seems awfully unfair not to be able to tell you about those wonderful boys.

(ROGERS *enters from the Press Room door.*)

ROGERS. Philip, for God's sake—(*breaks off*)—Daphne!

DAPHNE. (*She gives* ROGERS *her cheek to kiss.*) Oh, Joe, how are you, my pet? I'm so sorry, darling, I knew you'd be crazy with worry, but there was no way I could get a message to you, there really wasn't.

TEX. Where did you sleep?

HANK. What about the food?

DAPHNE. It wasn't so bad, truly it wasn't. They put me in a little cave, it was dark of course but I shouldn't complain, it used to be a wine-cellar or something, and they gave me some cotton-wool for my ears and anyhow they said the shells weren't landing anywhere near us at all, they said the German artillery is absolutely worthless, they can't hit a thing. They were so excited having an actress up there, they couldn't get over it. The Colonel was the wittiest man—you know what a sense of humour Americans have—he said to me, "War's odd, but this is the oddest it's ever been."

TEX. Did you sing to the boys?

DAPHNE. No, actually I didn't; as a matter of fact most of them were pretty busy, by busy I mean sleeping and shooting and oh you know and they looked so dirty poor things but of course I didn't see much of them because my room was lower down, but an awfully good-looking Captain came to talk to us, from Philadelphia he was.

(LEONARD *enters from hall door, carrying* DAPHNE's *mink coat.*)

LEONARD. Daphne!

DAPHNE. Oh don't be a stick-in-the-mud, Leonard. There's no harm in telling them a little about those wonderful boys.

LEONARD. (*stiffly*) Miss Rutherford is not free to give interviews to *anyone.*

ROGERS. I'd like to remind you that I knew Miss Rutherford before you did.

TEX. Now that she's a celebrity you can't expect her to limit herself to a small public.

LEONARD. (*furiously*) My public is *not* small. You might be interested to know that the Powermint Studios in Hollywood have cabled me to ask Miss Rutherford to star in a picture about Mount Sorello so she'll get all the recognition she so rightly deserves.

JANE. Wizard.

ROGERS. Well, I like that.

DAPHNE. Oh, Joe darling, I wanted to tell you myself, how could we know all this was going to happen and when Leonard first suggested it to me I said no I can't I really can't, poor Joe, and then he showed me a telegram from an American Senator saying the American public was deeply stirred to think an English girl had gone through all that to entertain American boys, and then came the Hollywood offer and Leonard said it was my duty to show people what had happened at Mount Sorello and since I was the only one who knew I had no right to refuse and I suddenly realized . . .

TEX. You shoving too, Leonard?

LEONARD. (*with dignity*) They want me to give technical advice on the script. I think this picture should be a realistic account of the Italian campaign and I'm very happy to be of service. Daphne, if we want to have lunch in Naples, we must be going.

DAPHNE. You *do* realize how it is, don't you, Joe? One minute you're a private individual and the next minute, well, you just don't seem to belong to yourself at all.

ROGERS. Sure. Forget it.

TEX. You wouldn't say a few words to us before you go, would you?

LEONARD. You *must* come, Daphne. (*ignoring others*) Goodbye, Major Brooke-Jervaux.

PHILIP. Goodbye, Lightfoot.

DAPHNE. Joe, dear, you don't want me to take a letter to your Mother, do you?

LEONARD. Daphne, there isn't time.

DAPHNE. Oh well, goodbye. I love you all, I really do.

(*Exit* DAPHNE *and* LEONARD.)

(CRAMP *enters from outside door.*)

CRAMP. The dispatch rider's here, sir.

HANK. Tell him to wait in front.

(*Exeunt* TEX, HANK, *and* ROGERS *via Press Room door, and exit* CRAMP *via outside door.*)

JANE. You know I'm really growing fond of Daphne. It was too enjoyable the way she stood Joe up. She certainly knows what she wants.

PHILIP. I think she's a dreadful woman. All she can think about is her silly career.

JANE. It isn't the career that's silly.

PHILIP. It seems so agitated and unnecessary, doesn't it?

JANE. Well, of course, she *is* an actress, even if she's a fool. It's her job.

PHILIP. Darling, sit down. (*He leads her to the sofa.*) It's lovely to have a minute alone with you. We don't have to worry about careers, do we?

JANE. It's almost too late for me to worry.

PHILIP. I go about in a daze, at least when I don't have to cope with their dreary dispatch riders, thinking of all the things we'll do at Frampton. It's probably quite different now, but after the war it'll be the same wonderful old life. It's going to be such fun to hunt together.

JANE. But, Philip, I don't know how to ride.

PHILIP. You've no idea what you've missed! Anyway, with Emily to teach you, you'll be hunting in no time. As a matter of fact, I've got the perfect horse for you. Easy to handle, and takes gates like a swallow.

JANE. You mean jumps over gates?

(PHILIP *smiles at her tone.*)

Wouldn't it be much better if I just got off and opened the gates?

PHILIP. Don't sound so frightened. The great thing is never to be afraid of horses. After a fall, you must ride again as soon as you're up and about. Emily took a pretty bad spill once and lay in a field an hour before anyone found her. . . .

JANE. You mean to say there's no one to pick up the wounded?

PHILIP. (*laughing*) You can't expect people to stop when they're with hounds. Oh, Jane, we're going to be so happy.

JANE. (*very small voice*) I'm sure we are.

PHILIP. We'll go to Scotland every year. I can't wait to take you. There's nothing as satisfying as fishing a stream with a light snow falling, and everything cold and quiet, and then the excitement of hooking them. Mother'll teach you how to tie flies. She's uncanny at it.

JANE. (*small voice*) That'll be awfully sweet of her.

PHILIP. Though perhaps really the most fun is the shooting.

JANE. You have to walk an awful lot, don't you?

PHILIP. Not duck-shooting! What a lazy girl! You'll sit in a blind with me, on the lake, and I'll bundle you up so you're very snug and warm and we'll make the greatest efforts to keep your feet dry.

JANE. (*cheered*) Just the two of us, in a little house on a lake? That sounds lovely.

PHILIP. It's not a house, darling, and you'll have to be terribly quiet or the ducks won't come in. It's the most wonderful feeling when the light begins to break and you hear the sound of their wings.

JANE. What time do you go on those shoots?

PHILIP. We usually start about four.

JANE. (*with horror*) In the morning, Philip?

PHILIP. You look so sweet when you're serious. I do adore you. . . .

(*He is leaning over to kiss* JANE *when*—ANNABELLE *comes in. She looks weary, her hair needs combing, her face is pale, and she is definitely discouraged.*)

ANNABELLE. Hello, chum. Hello, Major.

JANE. (*running to kiss her*) What was it like? You look awful. Was it ghastly? Did anyone get hurt?

ANNABELLE. (*drearily*) Tell you later.

JANE. It's all right. Philip knows.

ANNABELLE. Who told him?

JANE. Someone must have seen you and Dickie leaving town together. I don't know. It's okay, anyhow.

PHILIP. You're perfectly all right here, Miss Jones. I can't guarantee
what will happen when you file your story.

ANNABELLE. (*bitterly*) File my story!

JANE. It can't have gone wrong!

ANNABELLE. You know what I did? I sat. First in a shack, and then
in a tent. All day, and all night.

JANE. Weather?

ANNABELLE. The weather was past belief, but that wasn't it. Apparently they fly unless it's raining boulders. Something went wrong at the
other end. Dickie said probably the Germans were on to the landing-
strip.

JANE. They'll lay it on again, won't they?

ANNABELLE. Maybe. Dickie says it usually takes several weeks to re-
organize everything. It depends on the Poles. Oh, the pictures of wives I
had to look at last night. Wives, children, girl friends, and dogs. They're
all angels, but I'm worn to the nub.

JANE. Would a bath help?

ANNABELLE. What a pig I am! I ran into a couple of the sports
writers on the road and they told me about Daphne wrecking your trip.
It's the most maddening story I ever heard.

JANE. It's maddening all right.

ANNABELLE. (*fascinated*) Where is that stinker? What's happened
to . . .

PHILIP. Jane, you haven't told Miss Jones.

(JANE, *looking suddenly shy and rather uncomfortable, says nothing
while* ANNABELLE *waits.*)

(*proudly*) You'll be tremendously surprised—

(ANNABELLE *looks politely surprised.*)

Jane and I are engaged.

ANNABELLE. (*startled*) Good God, when did you have time?

(*collecting herself*) How lovely, darling. (*to* PHILIP) You're a very
fortunate man. Jane's always been the home-loving type.

JANE. Do shut up.

ANNABELLE. When is it?

PHILIP. Jane's going to Yorkshire to stay with my mother until we
can get married.

ANNABELLE. (*stunned*) How amazing. How lovely I mean. Well,
congratulations. I'm being awfully stupid; it really is a surprise.

JANE. Come on, I'll go up with you. You look like the end. You'll feel
better when you get a new face on.

(*Enter* ROGERS *via Press Room door as the girls turn to leave.*)

ROGERS. Annabelle! You're back.

ANNABELLE. I thought you were in Naples.

ROGERS. I thought you were in Poland.

ANNABELLE. You know about it, too.

ROGERS. Sure. I knew Hawkins' squadron was planning that trip.

JANE. Philip, I'm going up to pack. I'd like to talk to you a minute.

PHILIP. What's happening now?

(THEY *exit via hall doorway.*)

ROGERS. You must have a great story. Have you filed it yet?

ANNABELLE. I didn't go. The trip was called off.

ROGERS. (*brightening and affectionate*) Poor baby, what lousy luck. (*He sits down on sofa and puts his arm around her. She tries to draw back.*) You must be terribly disappointed. I'm so relieved you're safe I can't think of anything else. I've been sweating it out for twenty-four hours.

ANNABELLE. Now that Miss Rutherford's back from the garrison, having botched Jane's trip, I daresay you won't be so unhappy. Where is she, anyway?

ROGERS. Naples.

ANNABELLE. When are you joining her?

ROGERS. I'm not.

ANNABELLE. I thought you were going to be married.

ROGERS. I couldn't go through with it. I told her so when she came here this morning.

ANNABELLE. You mean you chucked her?

(JOE *nods.*)

I can't say I was crazy about her, but that seems pretty tough.

ROGERS. She'll get over it. She's young, she has lots of time. I admit I felt like an awful heel. At first I thought there might be a scene, but she took it pretty well. Here, put your feet up. You'll be more comfortable. (*He picks up her legs so that she is stretched out on the sofa. She protests, but he goes right on talking and sits down facing her.*) Anyway, it's all your fault.

ANNABELLE. Mister Rogers, I'm not going to have this blamed on me.

ROGERS. You must know why I dished Daphne.

ANNABELLE. Because she's a cracking bore.

ROGERS. There you go. The cattiness of women! That wasn't the reason at all and you know it.

ANNABELLE. I'm really not interested.

ROGERS. The moment I saw you I knew there'd never been anyone else.

(*He takes her hand and she pulls it away.*)

ANNABELLE. I think we'd better keep this on a straight basis of friendship.

ROGERS. Tell me if there's someone else, Annabelle. I'll understand. It's perfectly normal. Any man would try for you.

ANNABELLE. You must be thinking of some other girl. People have been awfully sweet to me, that's all.

ROGERS. That's it then. You might have told me. It isn't very honest to let a man love you if you're not interested.

ANNABELLE. I didn't say . . .

ROGERS. No, but I know what you mean. I wouldn't have believed you could, Annabelle, not after all we've had together.

ANNABELLE. I didn't . . .

ROGERS. Does he love you the way I do? The way you talk, the things you say, how mad you get, the lost causes. Or does he just think you're a beautiful woman—like any other beautiful woman?

ANNABELLE. There isn't any *he!*

ROGERS. There isn't? Oh, darling, I know I don't deserve you, but I love you so much. I want you more than anything in the world.

ANNABELLE. (*uncertainly*) It wouldn't work. We've tried it once.

ROGERS. The reason it didn't work was that I cared too much. I was always trying to keep you from getting yourself shot. If you try it again, I'll never interfere. I'll sit at home and sew purple hearts all over your uniforms.

ANNABELLE. (*laughing*) Since I never seem to get where I'm going, I shouldn't think you'd be awfully busy.

ROGERS. Oh, honey, you're still disappointed about Poland. You'll make the trip some time. Hawkins is bound to try it again, isn't he?

ANNABELLE. (*shaking her head*) He says probably not for weeks.

ROGERS. No other girl would have dared fly that mission. That's what I mean about you. You're everything. You're pretty and funny and brave. I think being so brave is one of the things I'm proudest of.

ANNABELLE. Joe! You've never talked like this.

ROGERS. I didn't want to encourage you. You do enough crazy things. But I've got to make you understand. Nothing means anything without you.

ANNABELLE. You didn't give Daphne that impression.

ROGERS. A man can be lonely, you know. (*rising*) I see it's no use. I'm sorry if I was boring you.

ANNABELLE. You're not, Joe. Only we can't make the same mistake all over again.

ROGERS. (*ignoring her*) You can't help it if you don't care about me. I see that. It's just that needing you the way I do, I hoped you might feel the same, but let's not talk about it any more.

ANNABELLE. If I thought you meant that . . .

ROGERS. I don't want you to be sorry for me. That's the last thing I want. I'm shoving in the morning, so I won't be bothering you any more.

ANNABELLE. I thought you weren't going to Naples.

ROGERS. I'm not. I'm going over to Capri for a few weeks. I've got a vacation coming.

ANNABELLE. Is it still lovely?

ROGERS. There's a pretty good Air Force hotel. It won't be very exciting, but I'll take a lot of books.

(ANNABELLE *picks up a cigarette and waits.*)

(*starting for the door*) Well, goodbye, Annabelle.

ANNABELLE. (*softly*) I'll miss you.

ROGERS. (*returning to her quickly*) How much?

(ANNABELLE *fumbles to light her cigarette, making time.*)

(*blowing out the match*) Don't light that.

ANNABELLE. Why not?

ROGERS. It will get in the way. (*He takes her to his arms and kisses her.*) Don't ever leave me again.

ANNABELLE. It's a lot of trouble for nothing, isn't it?

(*He kisses her again.*)

ROGERS. We're older now. We've learned what's really important. We won't let anything separate us.

ANNABELLE. (*Settling herself blissfully in his arms.*) Nothing.

ROGERS. We're going to Capri right now. We've lost twenty minutes already. (*He gets up.*) Will it take you long to pack?

ANNABELLE. No time at all.

ROGERS. You get your things, and I'll fix transport at the motor pool. Cramp can dig up some sandwiches and we'll eat lunch on the way.

ANNABELLE. I do *love* being arranged for.

ROGERS. (*kissing her lightly*) Are you happy?

ANNABELLE. Madly happy.

ROGERS. (*kisses her again, more intently*) Hurry, darling. We can do all this much better at Capri.

(ROGERS *exits via street door.*)

(ANNABELLE *hastily straightens her hair and adjusts her lipstick. As she is doing so,* JANE *enters from hall doorway with her arms full of stockings and underclothes which she dumps on the floor.*)

JANE. You'll have to help me sort them out. Not that it would break one's heart to get the wrong khaki underpants.

ANNABELLE. Of course I will. (*She flings her arms around* JANE *and hugs her.*)

JANE. Don't bother to tell me. I can guess.

ANNABELLE. We're going to Capri. He was so sweet. You can't quarrel with people in war-time can you? I don't know how to explain it, but he seemed so mixed up and lonely, and I suddenly realized what a rotten time he'd been having.

JANE. You're mad about him.

ANNABELLE. He absolutely gets me. I can't help myself.

JANE. You're sure it's not going to be the same old merry-go-round?

ANNABELLE. No, that won't happen again. He says so himself. And anyhow he's changed, Jane. He even said he was proud of me. I couldn't believe it.

JANE. Will you marry him?

ANNABELLE. No, it's too dangerous. You risk ruining everything with marriage.

JANE. (*moodily*) I see your point. Where did these evening stockings come from? I haven't had any for years.

ANNABELLE. R.A.F.[20] Gunner.

JANE. Men have such mistaken ideas.

ANNABELLE. Of course when they try to think they're hopeless.

JANE. I didn't mean that. I meant the things they actually enjoy doing. For fun. It seems unbelievable.

ANNABELLE. What's the matter? Has Philip got a lot of grim hobbies?

JANE. All he wants to do, after the war, is go back to the wonderful old life in Yorkshire. I can't tell you what it's like. Hunting, shooting, fishing.

ANNABELLE. You're a city girl, that's your trouble. It sounds like a very pleasant way to spend one's time.

JANE. Oh it does? Well, have you any idea what it means? It means getting flung from half-wild horses while they leap over gates like swallows. Then you lie in a field until you rot. They never thought of a field dressing station. Or else you're cowering in a wet little box on a lake, speechless, in the middle of the night, waiting for some silly ducks to show up. Or for real fun you go fishing somewhere in Scotland in a blinding snowstorm.

ANNABELLE. (*laughing*) Do you have to do all that?

JANE. It's not funny. It's all right for you to laugh. You'll be in a lovely dry dug-out somewhere.

ANNABELLE. (*laughing*) It's so unlike you to pay attention to what a man says. They never get things right.

JANE. He ought to know what goes on in his own country.

ANNABELLE. If I know you, nobody, not even Philip, will ever get you on a horse or up before dawn to shoot ducks.

JANE. I wish I felt so confident about it. He orders me around already, and I obey like a spaniel.

ANNABELLE. You do love him don't you? You oughtn't to do this unless you feel fairly enthusiastic about it.

JANE. I feel sort of wobbly every time I look at him.

ANNABELLE. He is attractive. I suppose you have to marry him? You couldn't get him any other way?

JANE. Oh no, I wouldn't dare suggest it.

ANNABELLE. You'll manage him all right. Men never really hunt or fish or shoot as much as they talk about it. You'll have lots of time to yourself.

JANE. During which time his mother will teach me how to tie flies.

ANNABELLE. Nonsense. During which time you'll write books.

JANE. I hadn't thought of that.

ANNABELLE. Don't argue about anything with him now, and when you get there, find the best room in the house and start writing.

JANE. I've been thinking of a novel for almost three years.

ANNABELLE. Well, you see. It doesn't matter about the shirts. They're all so horrible.

JANE. No, your sleeves are longer. Do find yours. And then if I have to clamber around the countryside a bit, it won't be so bad, because I'll be with Philip.

ANNABELLE. Of course, darling.

JANE. The outlook isn't too dark, is it? I was awfully depressed.

ANNABELLE. (*full of assurance*) It's always depressing when you're about to be married. That's only natural.

(*Enter* ROGERS *from Press Room door, carrying musette bag and type-writer.*)

ROGERS. Annabelle, you're terrible. The car's coming in fifteen minutes. (*picking up a khaki rayon petticoat*) You don't wear this, do you?

JANE. (*with dignity*) And why not? Don't you bother with underwear?

ANNABELLE. (*rising*) I'll be ready, darling.

ROGERS. Jane, make her hurry. She's never ready.

JANE. The voice of the master.

                    (THEY *both hurry out, their arms full of clothing.*)

(ROGERS *sits down in a chair and begins to read a magazine; gets up and goes behind bookcase and takes a drink; returns to sofa and sits down.* CRAMP *enters.*)

CRAMP. Have you seen Miss Jones, sir? There's a jeep outside.

ROGERS. Whose jeep?

CRAMP. The driver says Major Hawkins sent it.

ROGERS. What for?

CRAMP. I don't know, sir. He said to tell Miss Jones Major Hawkins said everything was on again and to hurry. He said she'd know what he meant.

ROGERS. Oh! (*pause*) Don't bother, Cramp. I'll tell her. I think she's upstairs.

                                                          (CRAMP *exits.*)

(ROGERS *walks up and down thoughtfully. Then he starts toward the door leading up to* ANNABELLE'S *room. He stops and paces up and down again. Then he starts towards the other door. He stops and takes out a cigarette. He fumbles for matches, puts the cigarette back into his pocket, quickly goes to* PHILIP*'s desk and writes a note. He folds and addresses it, and leaves it in the middle of the table. Then he picks up his musette bag and typewriter. As he is leaving,* PHILIP *enters from the Press Room door.*)

PHILIP. Going somewhere?

ROGERS. Just going to see a man. Be back.

(HE *exits.*)

(PHILIP *crosses to put papers in file on bookcase and* JANE *enters from hall door.*)

JANE. I'm all packed. I hope you appreciate the way I obey you.

PHILIP. It's been hours since I saw you. Sit down and talk to me. It's infuriating the telephone lines have to be down when I want to spend every minute with you. I've been poking through my kit for a picture of Frampton, but I've lost it. I did find a letter of Emily's though. (*He searches through his pockets.*) Damn, I must have left it in my room. Everything's in such an uproar today. It was so amusing. You know everyone's called up, so she and Mother practically run the place.

JANE. (*Genuinely shocked at this hardship.*) But how appalling for them!

PHILIP. Oh no, they couldn't be jollier about it. They think it's great fun.

JANE. Do they have to do all the housework?

PHILIP. No, there are a couple of elderly maids still hanging on, but Mother and Emily do the heavy stuff. Emily's got a passion for making butter and cheese. You know Cheddar cheese takes eight hours, but she says she's so good at it now she's using the time to re-read Trollope. (*laughs*)

JANE. (*hollowly*) Goodness.

PHILIP. They've had trouble with the cows. I must really write today. Emily was quite worried in the last letter. Four of the cows had mastitis.

JANE. (*anxiously*) Did they?

PHILIP. Mother looks after them. It's the plague of the dairy you know. Emily says Mother is brilliant with cows.

JANE. It's awfully clever of her to have learned.

PHILIP. Well, you know, they have to. Can't let things go to pieces, after all. Emily took up bee-keeping for Mother's sake.

JANE. Does your mother like bees?

PHILIP. No, darling, it's to have honey. She loves sweets and it was the only way. I must say Emily's too funny about it. You see you can't get the equipment now, since the war.

JANE. What equipment?

PHILIP. Gloves, and a mask, for handling bees. So she says she ties up her trouser legs so the bees won't creep in, and plunges on them.

JANE. (*horrified*) I don't believe it.

PHILIP. Oh yes, she's got lots of hives. She says bees can tell if you're afraid of them. It's only a question of courage. She hasn't been stung much, actually, so I suppose she's right.

JANE. (*uncertainly*) What do they do the rest of the time?

PHILIP. How do you mean?

JANE. I mean when the cows and the bees are asleep?

PHILIP. (*laughing*) Well, they're fairly tired I expect, at the end of the day. They get up at five or six in the morning, and they have committees and war jobs. I wouldn't worry about them; they've no time to be bored. I wish I had that letter here; you'd love it.

JANE. (*pulling herself together with an effort*) Philip, I've thought of something to do in Yorkshire.

PHILIP. I knew you'd take an interest. It's sweet of you to be enthusiastic even before you get there.

JANE. It's not exactly anything to do with Frampton. I mean I thought it would be a wonderful chance to write.

PHILIP. But, darling, nothing happens there, unless you want to cover the Church bazaar and the market fairs.

JANE. No, of course not, Philip. I meant books. Novels.

PHILIP. I don't want you sitting in a stuffy room typing all day. I want you to get out in the open, and enjoy yourself. All that business of writing and earning money is over. I'm looking after you now. (*He rises.*) I've got to take these papers to transmissions. Be back in a minute.

(*As he exits*

ANNABELLE *comes running in.*)

ANNABELLE. Has Joe come in?

JANE. I haven't seen him.

ANNABELLE. It's so typical. He rushes me off my feet, and then he's late.

JANE. (*dully*) He says he doesn't want me to, Annabelle.

ANNABELLE. Who says what?

JANE. Philip. He says he doesn't want me to write books. He wants me to stay out in the open.

ANNABELLE. Oh, you didn't tell him, did you? You shouldn't have done that.

JANE. (*moodily*) Have you ever nursed diseased cows?

ANNABELLE. Of course not!

JANE. That's what his mother does.

(ANNABELLE *begins to laugh but* JANE *does not see anything funny in it.*)

Have you ever grappled with bees barehanded?

ANNABELLE. (*still laughing*) I never heard of such a thing.

JANE. That's Emily's job. They fall into a sodden sleep at sunset because they're exhausted. You can't blame them.

ANNABELLE. (*gasping*) I'm sorry, darling.

JANE. I'm glad it amuses you to know that I'm going to be kicked by horses and stung by bees and finally die of mastitis from a cow.

ANNABELLE. (*trying to control herself*) We'll give you the finest funeral a girl could want.

JANE. That's large of you.

ANNABELLE. Fix your mind on all the lovely plumbing, and the beds with sheets.

JANE. My mind feels like a bottomless pit, around now.

ANNABELLE. You know you'll do exactly what you want, when you get there. And Philip will love it. Do you think I could pinch one of his cigarettes?

JANE. (*dully*) Help yourself.

(ANNABELLE *crosses to desk and sees a note addressed to herself.*)

ANNABELLE. How odd. (*She reads it.*)

(JANE *can tell from* ANNABELLE*'s face that something terrible has happened*)

JANE. (*alarmed*) Annabelle! What is it?

ANNABELLE. (*reading in a stony, controlled voice*) "Hawkins sent for you, but it's too dangerous. I love you too much. It doesn't matter for a man. P.S. Back tomorrow."

JANE. (*awed*) I wouldn't believe anybody could do a thing like that.

ANNABELLE. (*still stony-voiced*) No one except Rogers.

(*Suddenly she crumples up the paper and throws it from her. Her voice chokes with tears of anger.*)

The crook. The lying crook. He never meant a word he said.

JANE. Oh, darling, it's too filthy!

ANNABELLE. He doesn't care what he does to me. He doesn't care about anything except getting his stories on the front page. It isn't even as if he liked the Poles.

(JANE *is walking up and down, thinking.*)

JANE. (*excited*) We're crazy. Dickie won't take him.

ANNABELLE. (*cheering up at once*) You think so?

JANE. Why should he? It was *you* he wanted to take. (*suddenly doubtful*) Oh! That note!

ANNABELLE. What note?

JANE. The one you wrote to Dickie yesterday morning. What did you say in it?

ANNABELLE. Nothing, except that I was heartbroken I couldn't go, and good luck.

JANE. Joe has it.

ANNABELLE. He can't have.

JANE. He has though. He swiped it from our room. Dickie will think you gave it to him to go in your place.

ANNABELLE. Oh, the swine! He's nothing but a common thief!

JANE. Can't we telephone Dickie's field?

(ANNABELLE *goes at once to the field telephone on* PHILIP*'s desk.*)

ANNABELLE. Operator, get me Trumpet through Grasshopper. What? How can they be? (*to* JANE) The only lines open are from here to Corps and here to Caserta.

JANE. Ask him if he's sure.

ANNABELLE. Are you sure, Operator? (*She listens and hangs up. To* JANE, *utterly discouraged*) He says that not being a deaf, blind moron he is sure.

(*There is a silence. Suddenly* ANNABELLE *turns her head away and it is seen that she is crying.*)

JANE. Oh, darling, don't. He's not worth it, you're lucky to know what he is, really, darling, he's such a pig you mustn't.

ANNABELLE. I believed him again, that's what hurts. I thought it was going to be lovely and I believed every lying word he said. It's so mean.

(JANE *stands by helplessly. Suddenly* ANNABELLE *straightens up.*)
I'm going to get out of here. I'm never going to see that stinking man again as long as I live. "Be back tomorrow," will he? He can come back everyday for ten years. He's not going to find me waiting.

JANE. (*timidly*) It would be lovely if you'd come with me. We could keep each other company. Maybe we could both write a book.

ANNABELLE. Thank you, darling. I'm going on with this war. I'm not going to let any worthless man ruin my job.

JANE. That's the way to talk. Where will you go?

ANNABELLE. (*She has started to collect her handbag and coat.*) I'll decide on the way to Naples.

(CRAMP *enters with a pile of letters which he leaves on the sideboard.*)

ANNABELLE. Cramp, will you bring down my luggage and put it in the command car Mr. Rogers ordered?

CRAMP. We'll be sorry to lose you, Miss.

ANNABELLE. You're the nicest man in this unlucky place, Cramp. You've been an angel.

CRAMP. (*beaming*) Thank you, Miss. I'll fetch your things.

(*Exit* CRAMP *via hall doorway as telephone rings.* JANE, *being nearest, answers it.*)

JANE. Who? Oh, hello, Pinkie, it's Jane. How are you, darling? What a bore. (*to* ANNABELLE) He's been trying to get us for twenty-four hours. I didn't hear. You're at Caserta? Is it nice? You're what? I can't hear at all. India? Why, Pinkie, what a change. What happened? (*to*

ANNABELLE) I haven't the faintest idea what he's talking about. Marvelous parties in Calcutta? I bet they are. You'll have a lovely time. When are you leaving? (*to* ANNABELLE) Today. Who? Me and Annabelle? Oh, I can't, darling. I've got to go to England. Yes, must. I don't know about Annabelle. (*to* ANNABELLE) You want to go?

ANNABELLE. (*Shaking her head*) I've really got to cover a war somewhere. Anyway, I haven't travel orders.

JANE. Annabelle can't either, Pinkie. Anyway, she hasn't any travel orders. (*to* ANNABELLE) Ever hear of a thing called O.C.G.?

ANNABELLE. Orders Commanding General. That passes over P.R.'s and everybody.

JANE. (*impressed*) Are *you* the Commanding General, Pinkie? Well, for goodness sake! (*to* ANNABELLE) He's got his own plane.

ANNABELLE. It does sound like fun. If I didn't have to work . . .

JANE. Annabelle says she'd adore to, but she really must cover a war somewhere. (*pause*) Why didn't you say so? (*to* ANNABELLE) India's only en route; he's going to Burma, he's going to be the big shot out there. What? (*pause*) But how *horrible!*

ANNABELLE. What is it?

JANE. Wait a minute. I'll tell Annabelle. (*holding receiver*) It's too awful. Those men have been away from home longer than anybody and nobody cares about their war. They call themselves the "Forgotten Army."

ANNABELLE. How unfair!

JANE. What did you say, Pinkie? (*to* ANNABELLE) Leeches, jungle sores, heat, fever, terrible casualties. He says you could be of great service.

ANNABELLE. Of course, I'll do anything.

JANE. He'll give you all facilities, transport, absolute freedom, everything.

ANNABELLE. Let me speak to him. Pinkie, this is Annabelle. When are you leaving? Right away? How will I get to you? Yes, at once. An hour and a half, I should think. Yes, I'll say goodbye to her. (*puts down the receiver*) He's holding the plane.

JANE. I must say that's stylish.

ANNABELLE. It sounds too terrible. Those poor men, and no one to tell what they're doing. Forgotten Army. How dare people treat them like that.

JANE. Oh, Annabelle, I'm going to miss you. Please come to Yorkshire. (*She kisses her.*)

ANNABELLE. Of course I will, sweetie. I want to be a godmother.

JANE. (*wistfully*) Be careful of snakes.

ANNABELLE. (*quite gay*) They're safer than bees, chum. (*When seeing* JANE's *face, she kisses her again.*) You'll have a lovely life, I know you will.

(ANNABELLE *hurries out of the main door.*)
(PHILIP *enters from the Press Room with papers in his hand.*)

PHILIP. Darling! You look sad.

JANE. Annabelle's gone.

PHILIP. Cheer up, she's not dead.

JANE. Yorkshire sounds so far away, Philip.

PHILIP. It is far away.

JANE. I mean so far away from the war. I'm afraid I'll feel like the most awful slacker.

PHILIP. Slacker? What an idea! You're too sweet, with your conscience. Didn't I tell you Emily bosses the land girls in their district? Why, they get up at five in the morning, and plough, and help with the harvest, and take care of the stock and everything the men did. They practically feed England. Emily'll have you in the land army before you've been there a day, so stop worrying. (*He kisses her on the top of the head lightly and starts to leave.*) You won't even have to give up wearing a uniform.

(*Exit* PHILIP *via Press Room door.*)
(JANE *sits riveted with horror for two seconds, and then races to the window. There is the sound of a motor starting. At the top of her lungs she shouts:*)

JANE. Annabelle! Wait for me.

(*She hurries across the room to pick up her handbag and* CRAMP *comes in, evidently intending to collect the mail he has left on the sideboard.*) Cramp, will you bring my luggage down and put it in the car with Miss Jones.

CRAMP. It's already down, Miss. I had it ready for your car to Caserta.

JANE. Will you do something for me?

CRAMP. Anything you say, Miss.

JANE. Tell Major Philip I'm no good at writing letters, tell him I really wouldn't be of any use in the country, he'll know what I mean, and please to excuse me and thank him for everything, and—and—oh, Cramp, if I don't go at once I'll never go, and it wouldn't work.

(*She exits hurriedly,—with* CRAMP *looking mystified but wooden, following her.*
TEX *enters alone via the outside door, whistling a tune. He dumps his coat on the floor in the corner and turns on the radio which immediately breaks into furiously loud Italian opera. He turns it off. He sees the mail on the sideboard and glances through it. Enter* HANK.)

HANK. My God, those girls are in a stew. What do you think they're up to?

TEX. No idea.

HANK. Something we haven't heard about?

TEX. I wouldn't care. I'm sick of this war. There's a service message for Rogers.

HANK. Read it. Might be something we ought to know.

(TEX *opens the cable.*)

TEX. The poor bastard. Italy's bad enough, but that's the pay-off.

HANK. What?

TEX. Ordered to Burma. Oh, boy, not for old Tex Crowder.

HANK. Nothing interesting?

(TEX *shakes his head and puts the message back in the pile of mail.*)

HANK. Time for a little game?

TEX. Okay.

(THEY *sit down at* P.R.*'s desk and deal cards.*)

(*Enter* PHILIP.)

PHILIP. Do you mind if I sit here too?

(TEX *and* HANK *nod pleasantly, but do not move.*)

(*Enter* CRAMP.)

CRAMP. Could I speak to you a minute, sir?

PHILIP. Certainly. Go ahead.

CRAMP. It's rather personal, sir.

PHILIP. (*rising*) Oh, all right.

(*The telephone rings.*)

Hello. Major Brooke-Jervaux speaking. Oh, good morning, sir. Yes, everything's fine. (*rather sourly, though forcing a laugh*) No, no women missing today. Really, sir? Oh, I say, I'm frightfuly pleased. (*to* CRAMP, *pointing to his shoulder:*) Another pip.

(CRAMP *looks very pleased.*)

Yes, sir, that is good news. Yes, I was rather expecting a transfer. It will be good to see England again. What? But, sir, it doesn't make sense. There are only a handful of correspondents out there. Build morale? But, sir! Yes, sir. Of course, sir. I'll report tomorrow, sir.

(PHILIP *hands up receiver, looking ill.*)

PHILIP. (*to* CRAMP) Burma, Cramp. They don't care what they do to a man.

(*The card players go on playing unconcernedly as the curtain falls.*)

FINIS

1. ENSA = Entertainments National Service Association provided entertainment for the troops: the British equivalent of the American services' USO.

2. Lend Lease = The Lend-Lease Act, signed into law by President Roosevelt in March 1941, before the U.S. had entered the war, permitted the immediate provision of material aid to the war efforts of countries considered of vital interest to the U.S.

3. M.P. = Military Police.

4. MAAF = Mediterranean Allied Air Forces.

5. Molyneux = Captain Edward Molyneux, whose Paris couture house, established in 1919, was known for its classic elegance.

6. *Stars and Stripes* = newspaper started in London in 1942 published by and for U.S. military in all U.S. theaters of war.

7. Mannerheim Line = line of defense named after the Finnish field marshal Baron Carl Gustav von Mannerheim, which extended across the Karelian Isthmus between Finland and Russia.

8. El Alamein = Egyptian coastal village about 65 miles west of Alexandria captured after fierce desert battles in October and November 1942, ending in British victory over Rommel's army.

9. Schiaparelli = Elsa Schiaparelli (1890–1972), Italian-born Paris couturier whose innovative and amusing designs gained fashion headlines in the 1930s.

10. Maginot Line = French system of underground fortification that stretched for 200 miles from Luxembourg to Switzerland along the border between France and Germany.

11. Elsie de Wolfe = famous socialite interior decorator for the rich international smart set in the 1930s.

12. D.S.O. = Distinguished Service Order, a coveted British award for officers only.

13. AGO card = Adjutant General's Office; an official U.S. identity card.

14. Molotov's cocktail party = Vyacheslav M. Molotov, Soviet Minister of Foreign Affairs from 1939 to 1945, whose position during the war was second only to Stalin's.

15. Clausewitz = Karl von Clausewitz (1780–1831), Prussian general whose three-volume treatise *Vom Kriege* (*On War*) is a landmark work in military studies.

16. REME = Royal Electrical and Mechanical Engineers (British).

17. "Lili Marlene" = a German love song that became very popular in the Allied and German armies.

18. Unpress ex O'Reilly (etc.) = the correspondent is using "cablese," a money-saver since the cost of a cable was determined by the number of words in it.

19. AFHQ = Air Forces Headquarters.

20. R.A.F. = Royal Air Force.

"It's wonderfully easy to criticize, isn't it?" says Ralph Michael (as Major Philip Brooke-Jervaux) to Joyce Heron (playing the war correspondent Jane Mason). This photo accompanied the 2 January 1947 *New York Times* review of the play's Broadway opening on New Year's Day. (*Courtesy New York Times*)

Above. The *New York Times* featured this five-column illustration on the front page of the Sunday arts and entertainment section, 29 December 1946. The caption reads: "In the usual order, Gerald Anderson and Georgina Cookson, representing the British press, are greeted by a couple of cynical American war correspondents, Warren Parker and David Tyrrell. From 'Love Goes to Press,' the week's play bowing at the Biltmore Wednesday." (Courtesy *New York Times*)

Right. *Harper's Bazaar* featured this photo in the September 1946 issue with the caption, "Martha Gellhorn and Virginia Cowles, right, wife of Aidan Crawley, Socialist M.P., were both war reporters in Italy; have collaborated since on London's current hit, *Love Goes to Press.*"

Opposite. Martha Gellhorn at a Thunderbolt base just inside Germany at the time of the air lift over the Rhine, winter 1945. (*Courtesy Martha Gellhorn*)

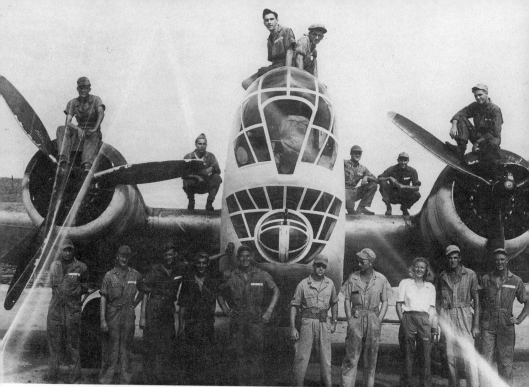

Above. Martha Gellhorn with the air and ground crew of a
B-18A bomber at the U.S. Air Force base at Borinquen Field,
Puerto Rico, in late summer 1942. Gellhorn accompanied the
flight crew on antisubmarine patrol. (*Courtesy Martha
Gellhorn*)
Above left. Martha Gellhorn, Cuba, 1941. (*John F. Kennedy
Library*)
Above right. Virginia Cowles, London, c.1941. (*Portrait by
Angus McBean, courtesy Cowles's daughter, Harriet Crawley*)

Afterword

When the movie *Thelma and Louise* was released in the spring of 1991, it unleashed a storm of controversy. What begins innocently when a wise-cracking waitress and bored housewife from Arkansas steal off on a weekend fishing trip results in their killing a would-be rapist in the parking lot of a roadside lounge. Our heroines suddenly find themselves on the run, with a newly acquired taste for the satisfaction of putting obnoxious men in their place, and we follow their reckless but exhilarating journey toward the Mexican border and self-discovery. *Thelma and Louise* was attacked for its gratuitous violence, for its poor female role models, and for deliberately presenting men in the worst possible light. (One critic labeled it "toxic feminism" and found in its "paean to transformative violence" an "explicit fascist theme.")[1] But others defended the film as a fresh twist on the genre of the "buddy film"—as a "road movie" with the difference that "this story's daring anti-heroes are beautiful, interesting women."[2] Nearly fifty years before Susan Sarandon and Geena Davis hit the road as Thelma and Louise, Martha Gellhorn and Virginia Cowles had created a similar pair of funny, daring, sexy, quick-witted—and, I hasten to add, entirely nonviolent—heroines in their World War II comedy, *Love Goes to Press*.

A romantic farce set in a press camp on the Italian front in 1944, *Love Goes to Press* was a success in postwar London. The review in the *Spectator* praised the play for its "gusto, astringency and much skilfully applied local colour."[3] The London *Times* review aptly outlines the plot:

> There are two heroines—both famous American correspondents, and they are as unlucky in love as they are lucky in war. One thinks of patching things up with a former husband, who made life impossible by appropriating her "scoops" for his own paper on the plea that the projected stunt was too dangerous for his little woman; and this time he does it again. The other falls in love with a p.r.o. [Public Relations Officer] for whom, naturally, newspapers have no existence apart from the war. He is a regular hunting, shooting, and fishing Englishman, as thick-headed as he is handsome, and when he gives the famous war correspondent some account of the rigours and dangers of life at his place in the country she pales with terror and flies away to another war in Burma.[4]

The play opened on 10 June 1946 at the Devonshire Park in Eastbourne for a week-long preliminary run before its London premiere.

The reviewer for the weekly theater newspaper the *Stage* gave the play high marks, commenting that "at times the humour rises to brilliance"—and the Eastbourne audience "showed their appreciation in no uncertain manner." (However, the reviewer noted a few production details still needing attention, remarking that "it is difficult to believe that none of the American characters chews gum.")[5] On 18 June 1946, *Love Goes to Press* opened at the Embassy Theatre in Swiss Cottage, North London (equivalent to off-Broadway at the time). Martha Gellhorn's hometown newspaper, the *St. Louis Post-Dispatch,* covered the opening night performance, noting that "throughout its three acts the play's authors, both well-known American newspaper women, sat nervously in the balcony," but while the actors answered a dozen curtain calls and the audience called for the authors, the authors "quietly slipped out of the theater."[6] The play delighted audiences for weeks at the Embassy, then moved to the Duchess Theatre in London's West End, where it ran for forty performances from 22 July to 24 August 1946. Its West End run was successful enough for the play and the principal members of its London cast (minus Irene Worth) to be moved to New York. The play was *not* a hit on Broadway. It opened at the Biltmore Theater on 1 January 1947. It closed on 4 January, thereby acquiring (in the words of the *Post-Dispatch*) "the combined doubtful honor of being the first play and the first flop of the year."[7]

The play was written as a joke. American critics didn't get it. While the *Theater Arts* reviewer was downright offended that two war correspondents could have demonstrated such "strange ethics" and "incredible human callousness," the *New Yorker* and the *New York Times* responded with sophisticated yawns.[8] "To the best of my knowledge, this was the first work to treat the late war on such frivolous terms," wrote the reviewer for the *New Yorker,* "and presumably it indicated that the time has come when we can properly consider the humorous aspects of Armageddon." But conceding that "this well may be a healthy sign," he considered it "a pity that the play itself couldn't have been a little better, especially since both authors are experienced military reporters and ought to have known what they were talking about."[9]

Indeed, by the time they wrote the play in 1945, Virginia Cowles and Martha Gellhorn had seen plenty of war. Virginia Spencer Cowles (1912–83) covered the Spanish Civil War in 1936 and 1937 as a free-lance newspaper correspondent, reporting from behind both Fascist and Republican lines. From 1938 to 1945, as a roving war correspondent for the London *Sunday Times* and the *Daily Telegraph,* she observed the Nazis up close in Berlin, witnessed from Prague the tragic breakup of Czechoslovakia, then covered the Russian invasion of Finland, the German invasion of France, the North African campaign, the Italian campaign, and the Allied invasion of France and Germany. Virginia Cowles chronicled her experiences and observations of wartime Europe in her book *Looking for Trouble*, a 1941 best seller. From 1942 to 1943 she served as special assistant to the American ambassador in London. At the time the play opened in London, she was newly married to Aidan Crawley, an English journalist who served in the Royal Air Force and was taken prisoner of war from 1941 to 1945, who went on to become a Labour Member of Parliament (1945–51), a Conservative Member of Parliament (1962–67), and a Member of the Order of the British Empire. After the war, Cowles went on to write fourteen more nonfiction books on historical figures and events, including biographies of Winston Churchill, Edward VII, the Astors, the Rothschilds, and the Romanovs. In addition to the vital statistics of her birth, marriage, children, and books, the formulaic write-up about her in *Who's Who* contains this nugget of information: "*Recreation:* politics."

By the time Martha Gellhorn got to the Spanish Civil War at the age of 28, she already had published a novel and a book called *The Trouble I've Seen* (1936)—four short novels of the Great Depression drawn from her observations as a field investigator for the Federal Emergency Relief Administration.[10] *The Trouble I've Seen* was a critical success and earned her the admiration of H. G. Wells (who wrote the preface) and the lifelong friendship of Eleanor Roosevelt. When Gellhorn wanted to travel to Spain in 1937 to witness the civil war, an editor at *Collier's* magazine helpfully provided her with a "to whom it may concern" letter stating that she was a special correspondent, although she had no connection with the publication. When she actually sent in a piece about wartime Madrid, they put her on the masthead.[11] From 1937 through the Second World War, Martha Gellhorn served as a war correspondent for *Collier's*, filing reports from Spain, Czechoslovakia, Finland, China, Singapore, Java, the Caribbean, England, Italy, France, Holland, and Germany. Before the war ended she also published a collection of short stories, *The Heart of Another* (1941), and another novel, *Liana* (1944). In her six-decade career as a journalist, short story writer, and novelist, Gellhorn has published fifteen books, and since World War II she has gone on to report on wars in Vietnam, the Middle East, and Central America. In the winter of 1990 at the age of 81, she cut short a snorkeling trip in Belize to travel without credentials and at her own expense to witness the results of the U.S. invasion of Panama; her report appeared in the Spring 1990 issue of *Granta*.[12]

The *New Yorker* reviewer of *Love Goes to Press*—the one who thought that two such experienced military reporters as Martha Gellhorn and Virginia Cowles "ought to have known what they were talking about"— found it troublesome that "with so much material at their disposal, . . . the ladies mysteriously decided to focus on love."[13] Brooks Atkinson of the *New York Times*, also acknowledging that Gellhorn and Cowles "know the racket as well as a few of the most celebrated operators whom they satirize," similarly charges that "*Love Goes to Press* is not the cartoon that two frisky artists ought to draw of the typewriter soldiers. As the title indicates, they waste most of the evening on some dull and profitless love affairs." "But," he pronounced authoritatively, "love will have to fly out the window when the real satire of war correspondents gets written"—as though there were a universal and undisputed standard for the genre ("satire of war correspondents" being a rather exotic subspecies at that).[14]

These criticisms are grounded in the play's failure to meet the reviewers' criteria (unstated) for drama set in wartime. *Love Goes to Press* conforms to no familiar patterns. Yet what the American critics of Gellhorn and Cowles's wartime comedy seemed to find inherently boring—"affairs of the heart that need not detain you this morning," as Atkinson put it—is precisely what seems to me most interesting about the play.[15] *Love Goes to Press* portrays men and women in love and at war from a distinctly female point of view, a lens through which we rarely have had the opportunity in American literature to view the Second World War, or any war. And in this wartime drama, the European Theater of Operations is literally that—the stage set for the main action: the War between the Sexes.

The correspondents at the play's fictional press camp are characteristically competitive, but when two women reporters show up we witness instant male bonding. Learning of the impending arrival of the "internationally known, glamourous war correspondent" Jane Mason, Major Philip Brooke-Jervaux, the public relations officer, is incensed, anticipating untold disruptions and inconveniences and believing that "any decent woman would stay at home." Unaware that Jane is about to be joined by fellow correspondent Annabelle Jones—her old war buddy and his own ex-wife—the reporter Joe Rogers is caustic: "I'm allergic to newspaper women. I married one once. They never stop trying to scoop you, and when you scoop them they divorce you." (Annabelle's version of the marriage is rather different: "It turned out he married me to silence the opposition.")

While Jane and Annabelle live up to their reputation for glamour, they are at the same time legendarily fearless and successful war correspondents—in marked contrast to their male counterparts in the play, who, when not actively filching the work of others, feed their newspapers warmed-over military briefings and limit their interviews to nearby cooks and jeep drivers, quoting them as high-ranking Allied officials. Predictably, the men whom they threaten to outshine cry foul and attribute the hard-earned successes of the "girls" to their sex appeal.

The fact is, of course, that being female is a definite occupational handicap for a war correspondent, and both Jane and Annabelle know it. But because their womanhood is something that they have never been allowed to forget, they have great fun flaunting it. With a perfect understanding of the currency of power, they turn a handicap to their own advantage in repeated acts of subversion that the authors exploit to comic effect. These feminist heroines literally do wear combat boots, but they bring lipstick to the front as well, and they never lack for an "errand brigade" of willing men to carry their luggage.

Gellhorn and Cowles's heroines rupture stereotypes from all directions: they are crack correspondents, but they are not simply "hardboiled" career women; they certainly are not victims, but they *are* at times vulnerable. And as much satisfaction as they take in their work, they need love as well. Like most real people, Jane and Annabelle are contradictory characters whose personal and professional lives sometimes pull them in opposite directions.

Again, critics responded differently on each side of the Atlantic. The English reviewer for the *Spectator* was understanding: "If, when the tender passion intervenes to blur the heroines' professional objectives, a certain unreality obtrudes itself, that is after all (the two ladies might argue) only what happens in real life; and in any case it makes little difference to our enjoyment of a most competent play which is admirably acted and produced."[16] But the *New Yorker* reviewer was less tolerant of life's ambiguities, finding it troublesome that, "while the authors were occasionally able to see their characters as a couple of good, hearty comics, they were unable to get away from the contrary notion that the girls were also talented, sensitive, and pretty damn picturesque figures, of some serious dramatic consequence. The result was a blend of the glamourous and absurd that may, I suppose, easily have been the truth but was moderately confusing on the stage just the same."[17] Presumably he would have been more comfortable had the "girls" stayed put in their two-dimensional places.

The controversy surrounding *Thelma and Louise* testifies to just how far ahead of their time Gellhorn and Cowles were in portraying two women making it in a man's world on their own decidedly female terms—acting unapologetically, if not extravagantly, like *women.* Janet Maslin, writing for the *New York Times,* suggests that what really rankled some about *Thelma and Louise* was "something as simple as it is powerful: the fact that the men in this story don't really matter. They are treated as figures in the landscape through which these characters pass, and as such they are essentially powerless. For male characters, perhaps, this is a novelty, but women in road movies have always been treated in precisely the same way. The men in this story may be boors or charmers, but in neither case do they have much effect on what Thelma and Louise do."[18] Similarly, in *Love Goes to Press,* the men serve mainly as plot accessories, figures in the landscape through which our heroines pass.

As I am hardly the first to point out, American literature contains a long tradition of stories of men without women. A central American myth focuses on a man alone, pursuing his quest unaccompanied by a woman—if not actively fleeing the domestic entanglement she represents. Returning home after his twenty-year sleep, Rip Van Winkle sadly learns that his old friends have passed on, but he finds "a drop of comfort, at least" in the news that his shrewish wife is also gone, having burst a blood vessel yelling at a New England peddler; Captain Ahab and the *Pequod* crew chase Moby Dick through the high seas with no woman in sight; and when Huck Finn learns that his Aunt Sally intends to take him home and "sivilize" him, he lights out for the Territory.[19]

What Martha Gellhorn and Virginia Cowles have created in *Love Goes to Press* is a world of women without men. Beyond the simple fact that it is good fun, and conceding that the authors intended it as a money-making joke, the play nevertheless is an important piece of women's literary history. Here *women* are the subjects; men, the objects of their speculations and desires. Gellhorn and Cowles reverse the male gaze. They present us with the equivalent of a locker room scene, but instead of watching the guys shower and shave while they talk about girls, we watch Jane and Annabelle cold-creaming their faces, folding their khaki laundry, and admiring each other's hairstyles while discussing the charms of various men about camp. But they have their priorities straight. When Annabelle asks Jane "How's your love life?" Jane replies, "Bad. I got slightly involved with a Frenchman in Tunis last summer, but then we invaded Sicily, and I had to leave him."

In *Love Goes to Press*, *women* are normal; men, the mysterious and baffling Other. Here the *women* think straight; men are silly, irrational creatures to be handled with gentle indulgence. When a smitten pilot expresses astonishment that "two little American girls" would want to do dangerous things like fly into Yugoslavia and go to the front when "any man would give his eyes just to take care of girls like you," the stage directions call for Jane and Annabelle to regard him "with complete loathing," talking to him "as to a poodle or a child." They express wonder that Joe Rogers could be interested in the dizzy actress Daphne, whom they consider a "cracking bore." But, as Annabelle says, men "see things in an odd little way of their own": "Of course when they try to think they're hopeless."

Thelma and Louise has been described as "'9 to 5' meets 'Easy Rider.'"[20] *Love Goes to Press* might be described as *9 to 5* meets *Huck Finn* with scenes from *A Room of One's Own*. The play reveals that the women's greatest fantasy is to be valued as much for their accomplishments as for their female charms, to be loved as much for their brains as for their bodies. Their intelligence and independence are precisely what make the play's heroines attractive to men, but each woman finds that, as soon as a man thinks he has won her, he wants to own her. For Jane, the main attraction in sitting out the rest of the war at Philip's Yorkshire farm is that "it would be a wonderful chance to write," to finally work on a novel, but Philip brushes off her plans as nonsense: "All that business of writing and earning money is over," he tells her. "I'm looking after you now." Annabelle, wiser from experience, has no intention of remarrying Joe—"You risk ruining everything with marriage," she tells Jane—but still she is shocked when, on the eve of their third "honeymoon," Joe not only stands her up and steals her trip to Poland but, to add insult to injury, claims to have done it to protect her.

In this story, for the woman who seeks fulfillment in both love and work, there can be no happy ending. Finally, the only way Thelma and Louise can escape their male pursuers and maintain their autonomy is to clasp hands in sisterhood and solidarity and drive their turquoise Thunderbird convertible off a cliff; the only way Annabelle and Jane can escape the clutches of domesticity and preserve their freedom is to light out for the Territory—in this case, Burma. But in the punch line of the play, both Philip and Joe receive orders to proceed to the same spot, and we realize that our heroines will not find blissful freedom there, either.

For the record, Martha Gellhorn has seen *Thelma and Louise* and thought it "great fun, wonderful—two pissed-off women going off and having some fun."[21] Yet, while the play prefigures that screen hit nearly five decades in advance, *Love Goes to Press* also is close kin to such forties movie classics as *His Girl Friday* (1940), starring Rosalind Russell and Cary Grant, and *Woman of the Year* (1942) and *Adam's Rib* (1949), starring Katharine Hepburn and Spencer Tracy. In these fast-paced comedies, what was known as a "New Woman"—smart, good-looking, and extremely competent in her chosen career—plays opposite a husband (or ex-husband) in the same profession and threatens to "out-man" him at his own game. Like *Love Goes to Press,* these screen comedies are broadly drawn, deploying contrived entrances and exits, mix-ups, mass confusion, mistaken identity, and rapid-fire verbal dueling as part of the fun. And, like the play, they also exploit gender stereotypes and role reversals to comic effect. (At one moment in *Woman of the Year,* Spencer Tracy, playing a sports reporter, is disgruntled to find himself in the kitchen frying eggs for his internationally renowned journalist wife and her male secretary.) But these New Woman comedies, all written and directed by men, end happily ever after when the contentious couple kisses and makes up. *Love Goes to Press* is a New Woman comedy with a unique difference: it was written by two New Women, and their idea of "happily ever after" does *not* include their mates.

The cutthroat competitiveness of journalists, here intensified and complicated by the matter of gender, is a major source of humor in *Love Goes to Press.* Martha Gellhorn was as intrepid a journalist as either of the play's fictional heroines. She saw a battalion of Finns in white camouflage overalls holding off divisions of the Red Army on the Karelian Front; she flew the 3,000-mile round trip between Hong Kong and the Burma end of the Burma Road in an unheated and unpressurized DC-2 of the China National Aviation Company, dodging Japanese bombing raids en route; in August and September 1942 she set off for six weeks in a thirty-foot potato boat—in hurricane season and amid German submarine activity—to report on Allied military operations in the Caribbean; and having lost her front-line credentials just before the D-Day invasion, she smuggled herself aboard an unarmed hospital ship by locking herself in the toilet and went ashore in France with the stretcher bearers on the night of 7 June 1944.[22]

And, like the play's heroines, she, too, often had to outwit the authorities to do her job. (As far as she was concerned, she says, there were two enemies in the war: the Germans and the American Public Relations Office.)[23] After D-Day she was threatened with deportation by London desk officers and banished to a nurses' camp in northern England, but she escaped at night, went to the nearest airfield, and caught a ride to Italy on a fighter-bomber by telling a pilot that she had to go there to see her fiancé who was dying of wounds. From then on she covered the war as a sort of outlaw hitchhiking correspondent, keeping one step ahead of the officials, until she reached the concentration camp at Dachau, where she heard the news of the German defeat.[24]

But in her introduction to the play Gellhorn warns that what goes on in the press camp at Poggibonsi bears no resemblance to real war or war correspondents. And on the issue of professional competition among journalists, she draws a clear distinction between the type of reporting she did for *Collier's* and the reporting of most other correspondents she knew, who worked for daily newspapers or wire services: "They had to get stuff in fast, and it was very important that somebody who was working for the AP should say they took Hill 242 twenty minutes before somebody working for the *Times*. They were really in a time competition, which I was not. I was working for a weekly, and I didn't care when I got the stuff in. It didn't make any difference to me." The kind of war reporting she did "didn't have to do with immediate news or any form of competition," Gellhorn explains today. "It had to do with trying to understand, to see and understand, what it meant to the people involved. And I wasn't setting out to be a famous war correspondent. I was setting out to learn something."

Gellhorn refuses any glorification of her role as a war correspondent or as a woman war correspondent. Although being female was a definite disadvantage with higher command, which wanted to stop her, with the soldiers at the rank of sergeant and below, "it was generally delightful," she says. They considered her "a jolly joke." With the exception of Ernie

Pyle, whom they liked because he put their names and addresses in the papers, soldiers, she says, often resented male war correspondents, wondering why they were writing instead of fighting; "Whereas nobody expected me to be carrying a rifle. By and large, I think they thought it was sort of funny." And she dismisses any suggestion that her work was noble or heroic:

> Somebody said to me something like, "A woman war correspondent. Oh, you were there." And I said, how about the civilians? They're all over the lot. They're women too—killed, and waiting to step on mines, and their houses destroyed. I mean, come on. The absolutely only difference was that I wanted to be there, which put me in a position not of superiority, but protection, as it were. Because at any given moment, I could have said, this is too bad; I'm leaving. And they couldn't. And how about the soldiers?

"I think vanity in these things is inexcusable," she says.

Martha Gellhorn recalls that during the war she never saw her published pieces in *Collier's* magazine. "And I can't tell you how indifferent I was," she says. "Because as far as I was concerned, selfishly, I wanted to know, and then I wrote it the best I could, and if anybody wanted to take it in, that was up to them. I had done my job by seeing or learning and writing it the best I knew and getting it in. And from then on, it was somebody else's show, and not mine."

As for what motivated her war journalism, when asked if she felt it a moral responsibility to tell the stories of people who could not tell their own stories, she replied, "No, that's too grand":

> I sympathized. I thought they were all having a perfectly horrible time. I blamed that war absolutely on the governments of the democracies who had failed to stop it. I despised them. I have never, with the sole exception of James Gavin, met a general that I would wish to have a hot meal with.[25] But the people who had it all laid on them—I had the greatest possible pity and sympathy with them. And all I wanted to do was describe what war was like for people to whom it happened. I don't know if that's moral or not. I don't know why you write. Is that a moral obligation? I think you write because that's what you know how to do. And you write always about what interests and concerns you. And in journalism—somebody said, "Well, why do you keep writing about wars?" And I point out, that's what we've got. That's the history of our time. And I have had this great feeling about the record. I want it somewhere.

And the record stands. *The Face of War*, a collection of Martha Gellhorn's war correspondence first published in 1959, has been translated into Dutch and German and was updated and republished for the fifth time in English in 1993.[26]

Literary critics and historians are beginning to take a closer look at the impact of the two world wars on twentieth-century literature. Some have suggested that traditional military culture exaggerates and polarizes our notions of what it means to be male or female, and much of the work of women writers of the Second World War in particular serves to expose and challenge prevailing myths of gender.[27] Gellhorn and Cowles's World War II play certainly does expose and upset gender myths, but in a highly unusual genre. Part comedy of errors, part English country-house farce, part *Woman of the Year,* part *Thelma and Louise*—*Love Goes to Press* is a fascinating piece of women's wartime writing and twentieth-century American literary history.

Five decades later, *Love Goes to Press* seems surprisingly contemporary. It was written to entertain, and it still does. The particular source of its humor—the role of women in the military and men's resistance to women at the front—is still a contested issue, still "news" in the nineties. In *Love Goes to Press* Martha Gellhorn and Virginia Cowles managed to create a work that was far ahead of its time, yet very much a product of its time. But Martha Gellhorn would disapprove of our taking the play so seriously: "It is a joke. It was intended to make people laugh and make money."[28] But it is a *good* joke, and it belongs on the record.

Sandra Spanier

1. John Leo, *U.S. News and World Report*, 10 June 1991, p. 20.

2. Jane Maslin writes in her review of the film: "Funny, sexy, and quick-witted, these two desperadoes have fled the monotony of their old lives and are making up new ones on a minute-by-minute basis. Their adventures, while tinged with the fatalism that attends any crime spree, have the thrilling, life-affirming energy for which the best road movies are remembered." ("On the Run with 2 Buddies and a Gun," *New York Times*, 24 May 1991, p.C1).

3. Peter Fleming, review of *Love Goes to Press*, by Martha Gellhorn and Virginia Cowles, *Spectator*, 21 June 1946, p.635.

4. Review of *Love Goes to Press, Times* (London), 19 June 1946, p. 6.

5. Review of *Love Goes to Press, Stage*, 13 June 1946, p. 5.

6. "Martha Gellhorn Co-Author of Play Acclaimed in London," *St Louis Post-Dispatch*, 19 June 1946.

7. "Martha Gellhorn's Play to Close after Four Days," ibid., 4 January 1947.

8. Rosamond Gilder, review of *Love Goes to Press* in "Rainbow over Broadway," *Theater Arts* 31 (March 1947), 18.

9. Review of *Love Goes to Press, New Yorker*, 11 January 1947, p. 47.

10. The four short novels that constitute *The Trouble I've Seen* are included in *The Novellas of Martha Gellhorn* (New York: Knopf, 1993), published in England by Sinclair-Stevenson as *The Short Novels of Martha Gellhorn* in 1991.

11. For an account of her beginnings as a journalist, see Martha Gellhorn, "The War in Spain," in *The Face of War* (New York: Atlantic Monthly Press, 1988), 13–17.

12. Martha Gellhorn, "The Invasion of Panama," *Granta* 32 (Spring 1990), 204–29.

13. *New Yorker*, 11 January 1947, p. 47.

14. Brooks Atkinson, review of *Love Goes to Press, New York Times*, 2 January 1947, p. 22.

15. Ibid., 22.

16. Fleming, 635.

17. *New Yorker*, 11 January 1947, p. 47.

18. Janet Maslin, "Lay Off 'Thelma and Louise,'" *New York Times*, 16 June 1991, Sec. 2, p. 11.

19. A classic statement of the case is Leslie Fielder, *Love and Death in the American Novel* (1960; rev. ed. New York: Anchor Books, 1992). Judith Fetterley extends the argument in *The Resisting Reader: A Feminist Approach to American Fiction* (Bloomington: Indiana University Press, 1978).

20. The film's producer, Callie Khouri, credits her husband, the writer and producer David Warfield, for originating what she thinks is the most accurate description of *Thelma and Louise.* Larry Rohter, "The Third Woman of 'Thelma and Louise,'" *New York Times,* 5 June 1991, p. C21.

21. Martha Gellhorn, interview with Sandra Spanier, 9 July 1992, Chepstow, Wales.

22. For Gellhorn's accounts of these war experiences, see "Bombs on Helsinki," "The Karelian Front," and "The First Hospital Ship" in *The Face of War;* and "Mr. Ma's Tigers" and "Messing about in Boats" in *Travels with Myself and Another* (London: Eland Books, 1978).

23. Gellhorn interview. Gellhorn's comments in following paragraphs regarding her experience as a war correspondent are also from this interview.

24. For her account, see Martha Gellhorn's afterword to *Point of No Return* (originally published by Scribner's in 1948 as *The Wine of Astonishment*) (Lincoln: University of Nebraska Press, 1995).

25. General James Gavin commanded the U.S. 82nd Airborne Division.

26. The fifth edition of *The Face of War,* with a post–cold war conclusion, was published in England by Granta Books in 1993.

27. Important recent works on gender, war, and twentieth-century literature include Sandra M. Gilbert and Susan Gubar, *No Man's Land: The Place of the Woman Writer in the Twentieth Century,* Vol. 1: *The War of the Words;* Vol. 2: *Sexchanges* (New Haven: Yale University Press, 1988); Shari Benstock, *Women of the Left Bank: Paris, 1900–1940* (Austin: University of Texas Press, 1986); Margaret Randolph Higgonet et al., eds. *Behind the Lines: Gender and the Two World Wars* (New Haven: Yale University Press, 1987); Helen M. Cooper, Adrienne Auslander Munich, and Susan Merrill Squier, eds., *Arms and the Woman: War, Gender, and Literary Representation* (Chapel Hill: University of North Carolina Press, 1989). For discussions of women's writing and the Second World War in particular, see especially Susan Gubar, "'This Is My Rifle, This Is My Gun': World War II and the Blitz on Women," in Higonnet et al., 227–59, and Susan M. Schweik, *A Gulf So Deeply Cut: American Women Poets and the Second World War* (Madison: University of Wisconsin Press, 1991).

28. See Introduction.